SO-AHK-195

Feb 27

Cloverleaf
assessment

Your Leadership Edge

Tools and Strategies for When Everyone Leads

ED O'MALLEY & AMANDA CEBULA

Your Leadership Edge: Tools and Strategies for When Everyone Leads
Ed O'Malley and Amanda Cebula

Published by Bard Press, Portland Oregon

Copyright © 2015 Kansas Leadership Center
All rights reserved
Printed in the United States of America

Permission to reproduce or transmit in any form or by any
means — electronic or mechanical, including photocopying and
recording, or by an information storage and retrieval system —
must be obtained by contacting the publisher.

Bard Press
info@bardpress.com — www.bardpress.com

Ordering Information
For additional copies, contact your favorite bookstore or email info@bardpress.com.
Quantity discounts are available.

ISBN-13: 978-1885167682
ISBN-10: 1885167687

THIS BOOK IS DEDICATED TO:

Ed's favorite people:
Joanna, Kate, Jack and Lizzie

and

Amanda's examples and support:
Rich and Lyn Hoffman and Alan Cebula

CONTENTS

INTRODUCTION BY ED O'MALLEY

I was sitting across from a retired Army colonel. The last several years of his career had been focused on developing a new approach to building leadership in the Army. Experience in Iraq and Afghanistan suggested new approaches might be needed.

For eight years I had been on a mission to build leadership too. Not leaders. Not people with fancy titles. But people who understood how to get stuff done. And not just any stuff. Leadership is mobilizing people to tackle the most pressing, daunting, wicked challenges: *the tough stuff.*

IN OUR OWN WAYS, IN OUR OWN CONTEXTS, THE COLONEL AND I HAD STUMBLED UPON SIMILAR IDEAS.

> ▶ *Leadership is an activity, not a position.*
> ▶ *Anyone can do it, anytime and anywhere.*
> ▶ *It starts with you and must engage others.*
> ▶ *Your purpose must be clear.*
> ▶ *It's risky.*

We both understood leadership is about mobilizing people to make progress on adaptive challenges*, the types of problems that —as opposed to technical ones —defy simple solutions and require us to change our own behavior and how we relate to others.

The colonel slid a thick, spiral-bound book across the table. It must have contained 300 or more pages. It described a new way of thinking about leadership he and his colleagues had developed for the Army. As I thumbed through the pages, with their small font, graphics and charts, I immediately felt a kinship to the ideas. We had taken two paths to similar conclusions about leadership.

He had "shown me his" and now I had to "show him mine." In a sheepish way, I pulled a small card out of my pocket and slid it across the table. He gave me a 300-page manual. I gave him a card that fits in your pocket.

The small card contained a simple framework for thinking about leadership. The card listed four competencies along with supporting ideas under each.

The man across the table had parachuted behind enemy lines, led men into combat and dedicated his career to our armed forces. I didn't know him well, but I was humbled in his presence. And I wanted him to give me an "atta boy!"

* The good people of Kansas and my dear friend Marty Linsky introduced me to this way of thinking.

I waited as he looked the card over, afraid he might politely dismiss both it and me.

Then he looked up and said, "You nailed it. This is it."

SO WHAT WAS ON THAT LITTLE CARD?
WHAT HAD WE NAILED?
WHAT HAD MADE THE COLONEL LOOK UP AND TAKE NOTICE?

First, KLC and the colonel's team share a similar definition of leadership. It's based on the work of Ron Heifetz and Marty Linsky. We agree that "leadership is mobilizing people to make progress on deep, daunting, adaptive challenges."

Second, KLC had whittled down 300 pages of Army doctrine to the five guiding principles listed earlier and the following four leadership competencies.

▶ *Diagnose Situation*
▶ *Manage Self*
▶ *Energize Others*
▶ *Intervene Skillfully*

The four competencies allow us (and you once you've finished this book) to turn a definition of leadership into clear and purposeful action. They allow us to see our leadership edge and, rather than be afraid of it, embrace it in our pursuit of making progress.

YOUR LEADERSHIP EDGE?

It's the title of this book, and by now you might wonder just why we call it that. Leadership is rare, but it's a skill, an advantage even, that can be developed through learning and practice. The principles and competencies we cover here can help you hone that skill and develop the leadership edge needed to successfully confront problems that exist for your organization, company or community.

The four competencies were born out of an intensive listening process used to create the Kansas Leadership Center — a unique endeavor I started in 2007. (My first book, "For the Common Good: Redefining Civic Leadership," co-authored with David Chrislip, tells the story of KLC.)

That listening and discernment process, along with insight from countless participants and colleagues since then, gave birth to the ideas explored in this book. Working in concert, these competencies and the dimensions within them create a way of being for anyone wanting to be successful at mobilizing others around daunting challenges as they explore their leadership edge.

HERE ARE SOME KEY IDEAS TO HAVE IN MIND AS YOU EXPLORE THIS BOOK.

LEADERSHIP AND AUTHORITY ARE DIFFERENT THINGS.
Leadership is an activity. Authority is a role. Sometimes those with authority exercise leadership. Often they don't. This doesn't mean authority isn't important or doesn't have a distinct purpose, but this book is about the activity of leadership. Our fondest hope is the ideas help you — whether you are an authority figure or not — mobilize others.

LEADERSHIP REVOLVES AROUND CHALLENGES AND OPPORTUNITIES. You need to know what the challenge or opportunity is that you're trying to mobilize people around. You'll hear us reference "your challenges" a lot. You might spend some time thinking about what these might be. (Need help? Just think about whatever concerns you the most about your organization, community, company, etc. Those are the things crying out for leadership.)

LEADERSHIP AND ADAPTIVE CHALLENGES GO HAND IN HAND.
Adaptive challenges exist in our hearts and guts. Adaptive challenges linger. Solutions are elusive. Progress on adaptive challenges requires people themselves to change. And helping (motivating, encouraging, inspiring, cajoling, etc.) people to change is what leadership is all about.

So, the colonel was impressed that we'd managed to boil leadership down to one pocket-sized card. Granted, with this book we move beyond that little card (although contact us if you want one; it's so great, it fits in your pocket!). Still, we are keeping it simple, complete with cartoons. We like cartoons.

Leadership isn't complicated; it's just hard to do. But the ideas are simple enough to illustrate with cartoons. You could read dozens of thick leadership books or attend countless seminars. Or you could think about the cartoons and ideas here. Our experience suggests keeping it simple is the way to go.

Enjoy the journey.

Don't take yourself too seriously.

Lead.

Onward!

[signature]

P.S. – You can join our community at *www.yourleadershipedge.com*. For a subscription, you get access to all sorts of additional information as well as the invitation to weekly video chats facilitated by Amanda Cebula, our faculty and me. More information is located in the back of this book. We hope to see you there!

The mind is capable of taking in extraordinary amounts of information. But too often we think we have a better understanding of a situation than we actually do. We give the data a cursory scan and then jump into action. Few people probe deeply enough to identify the smart risks that will lead to real progress.

We diagnose situations on two levels: surface and profound. Most of us spend our time on the surface, clarifying what we think we know and then reacting to these preconceptions.

It's hard to resist jumping into action. It's expected. We've trained a lifetime for it. We are proud of what we've learned. We are hired and paid for our expertise. But expertise is not enough when facing adaptive challenges. We have to observe and understand the situation from all angles.

PART 1

DIAGNOSE SITUATION

CHAPTER 1

DIAGNOSE SITUATION

Distinguish Technical and Adaptive Work

Try to slay an adaptive challenge with a technical solution and you'll find yourself facing a bigger challenge than before.

Our friends Ron Heifetz, Marty Linsky and Alexander Grashow believe the single biggest mistake when trying to exercise leadership is treating an adaptive challenge as a technical problem. We couldn't agree more.

Ron, Marty and Alexander wrote the books on the difference between adaptive challenges and technical problems. Read their great books to learn more or spend some time with Cambridge Leadership Associates, the firm Ron and Marty founded.

Technical problems live in people's heads and logic. They are susceptible to facts and expertise. Adaptive challenges live in people's hearts and stomachs. They are about values, loyalties and beliefs. Progress on them requires the people with the problem to do the work, because the work involves refashioning deeply held beliefs.

Back to the cartoon. Wielding a technical solution solves a technical problem. The same technical solution applied to an adaptive challenge just exacerbates the problem.

There is always pressure in a community, company or organization to see challenges as technical problems. We want to believe things can be solved quickly, easily and with as little time and energy as possible. In reality, most complex problems are really a mixture of technical and adaptive elements. By distinguishing between the two types of problems, we collect clues about how to address them.

Adaptive challenges require leadership. Technical problems require well-exercised authority and expertise. Adaptive challenges are those things that concern you the most, the issues that linger. Solutions are elusive. Even agreement on the problem is elusive. Adaptive challenges are about values and culture, security and vulnerability.

HERE ARE SOME EXAMPLES:

▶ A new manager is told to reorganize her department, which will mean layoffs for some, new responsibilities for others and fewer supervisors overall. The previous manager, although well liked in the department, was demoted for being unable to accomplish a successful reorganization.

THE TECHNICAL ELEMENTS INCLUDE: imagining new organizational charts, changing where people sit, creating new processes, crafting termination agreements, etc. These elements are important, challenging and far from the complete picture.

THE ADAPTIVE ELEMENTS INCLUDE: shifting loyalties from the old manager to the new, helping the staff see their part in the failed reorganization, raising morale despite shrinking the department, and increasing productivity in the face of significant disruption.

▶ A professor is frustrated with being a part of a long-stagnant department with declining enrollment, little collaboration between faculty, a shrinking budget and little recognition on campus.

THE TECHNICAL ELEMENTS INCLUDE: sharing the department successes more broadly on campus, creating an electronic newsletter to keep faculty up to date on the work of their colleagues, etc.

THE ADAPTIVE ELEMENTS INCLUDE: creating a true aspiration among enough faculty for something greater than now exists, cultivating a shared vision, generating commitment to work for the success of the department rather than just for individual success, etc.

DISTINGUISHING TECHNICAL AND ADAPTIVE

	TECHNICAL WORK	ADAPTIVE WORK
THE PROBLEM	... is clear	... requires learning
THE SOLUTION	... is clear	requires learning
WHOSE WORK IS IT?	experts or authority	stakeholders
TYPE OF WORK	efficient	act experimentally
TIMELINE	ASAP	longer term
EXPECTATIONS	fix the problem	make progress
ATTITUDE	confidence and skill	curiosity

HERE'S A BASIC WAY OF THINKING OF THESE TWO ELEMENTS:

TECHNICAL PROBLEMS:

can be solved by experts or authorities. Few people may be needed. Someone, somewhere has solved the problem before and a roadmap for the next steps exist. Best of all, many technical problems are quickly and easily solved.

ADAPTIVE CHALLENGES:

have a totally different feel. The conversation is circular. Movement on an issue is difficult to track. We usually need to learn exactly what the problem is and then how best to proceed. Stakeholders, not just authority figures, must work on adaptive challenges. With no clear roadmap, you must experiment to test possible ways of moving forward. Even the timetable is elusive.

WANT TO LEARN MORE ABOUT TELLING TECHNICAL AND ADAPTIVE WORK APART?
Read "Leadership on the Line" by Ron Heifetz and Marty Linsky or visit *www.cambridge-leadership.com.*

Need help identifying the adaptive challenges?
Ask your people five questions:

1. When you think about the future of your organization, department, team or community, what concerns you the most? (By focusing on "the most," people tend to articulate adaptive challenges.)

2. What makes progress difficult on this concern? (This identifies the big process challenges — hallmarks of adaptive work — which often need to be the real focus of acts of leadership.)

3. What type of leadership (attitudes and behaviors) will it take from all of us to overcome those barriers?

4. What makes that type of leadership difficult for you? (This helps drive home that exercising leadership on adaptive challenges isn't easy, and no one does it well all the time.)

5. What will it take to build more of that type of leadership within our group? (Implementing the answers to this question could bring significant progress on the adaptive challenges concerning people the most!)

What gets in the way of telling technical and adaptive work apart?

GIVE ME SUCCESS NOW!

Our culture drives us to produce quickly, clouding our judgment
and leading us to treat most things as technical problems that
can be solved quickly.

I WANT TO BE A HERO

Taking the time to distinguish technical and adaptive work means
I might be seen as someone just sitting around and not saving the day.

IGNORANCE

Many of us are simply unaware of these distinctions, so we can't
even contemplate distinguishing between the two.

MAKE IT REAL
Q&A

We're trying to establish an employee wellness program at work. Our company is committed to its success, but we're struggling to get started because we know there will be a lot of elements involved in implementing it. Where do we begin?

-WORRIED WILLIAM IN THE WELLNESS DEPARTMENT

Dear William,

Start by writing down the technical and adaptive elements of setting up a wellness program. The adaptive challenges are the ones that involve people's values and behaviors. At the top of the list of adaptive elements could be "discovering how employees currently approach wellness" and "finding out how open employees are to engaging in workplace wellness." If this were my project I'd also put "developing a team of champions" in the adaptive column. Our advice: Don't roll out a company-wide program until you have a group of influential people at all levels committed to success.

Onward!

CHAPTER 2

DIAGNOSE SITUATION

Understand the Process Challenges

Process challenges are people challenges.

Process challenges are issues or barriers among members of a team or organization. They are about how people work (or don't work) together. They exist regardless of the content challenges — the readily solvable nuts-and-bolts decisions and details — facing the group. Process challenges could be thought of as the problems behind the problems, or even the problems behind those.

The right people, with good information, in a
healthy process, create authentic, lasting results.
—DAVID CHRISLIP

Good politicians understand this instinctively. The issue isn't how to build the highway but how to create community support for it.

HERE ARE MORE EXAMPLES:

▶ A start-up company is developing a new technology to make lives better, but the founders are at odds, each having a different vision for the company.

CONTENT CHALLENGE = developing the new technology.
PROCESS CHALLENGE = reconciling two different visions.

▶ The year-end budget report is due by Friday. The boss asked for a new format with additional information to help management make better forecasts but didn't specify what should be in the new format. The budget team is struggling. The report has been the same report for years, since before any current staff were hired. The team members have no good ideas for how it should be different and are stressing about getting it done on time. They are not even sure why senior management want something different.

CONTENT CHALLENGE = new budget report.
PROCESS CHALLENGES = imagining a whole new way of presenting information, working under stress, uncertainty and lack of clarity between management and the budget team.

WANT TO LEARN MORE ABOUT PROCESS CHALLENGES?
Read "Buy-In" by John Kotter.

In "Hoosiers," the best basketball movie of all time, the main character's challenges are less about the content of basketball (e.g., which offense to run) than about the process challenges inundating him. He is a newcomer in town and isn't accepted. The players don't work together as a team. His experiences at another school affect whether a key individual will trust him. What he knows about the X's and O's of basketball is important but not sufficient. Navigating the process challenges is key.

▶ A community action group has rallied a neighborhood to speak with one voice about the need to replace the dilapidated school. Parents of young children, the elderly and single people are all in favor. But most school board members have a different perspective than the community group.

CONTENT CHALLENGE = building a new school.

PROCESS CHALLENGE = building bridges between the community group and the majority on the school board.

▶ A CEO lays out a new vision for her organization that she believes will keep the company relevant for years to come. The vision includes a new suite of services as well as a public relations effort.

CONTENT CHALLENGE = the stuff in the vision.

PROCESS CHALLENGE = helping staff and stakeholders embrace the vision — better yet, ensuring staff and stakeholders help inform the vision!

*To lead you must understand
the process challenges.*

Why?

*Because it's the process
challenges that derail so many
leadership efforts.*

**What makes it hard to understand
process challenges?**

▶ They seem like a sideshow, but they are the main event. It's more
fun to refine a new product (content challenge) than to face
problems among the co-founders (process challenge).

▶ It takes time and discernment to identify the process challenges.
Content challenges are usually easier to see. In our quest for a quick
fix, we get satisfied by working on the content challenges.

▶ Consciously or unconsciously, we don't want to uncover the real
problem. It just might be too messy.

Lessons from History

During World War II the race was on among the Americans, Germans, Russians and British to develop the atomic bomb. The best scientists in each country were assigned the task and massive amounts of materials were harnessed to conduct the research. The content challenge was to split an atom, unleashing its destructive force. In America, process challenges were abundant while the scientists were busy on that massive and complicated content challenge.

The Army and Navy each had separate research efforts, and it took years before they shared information and learning (PROCESS CHALLENGE). How information is shared is usually an important process challenge. Huge amounts of materials — from steel to chemicals — were needed, but those same materials were needed to produce tanks, ships and planes. Gaining enough influence over the supply chain to divert materials to their project was critical for the research teams (PROCESS CHALLENGE). Simply focusing on the content challenge — the splitting of the atom — wouldn't suffice.

How to understand the process challenges

▶ Build relationships with others. This is essential. The more you care about others, the more you share their perspectives.

▶ For a specific issue or project, ask this question: "As we are working on ＿＿＿ (insert name of project), what could really derail us?" The answers will usually be process challenges.

▶ For broader process challenges affecting a community or organization, ask this question: "When we think about the future of ＿＿＿ (insert name of community/company/etc.), what concerns you the most?" Then ask, "What makes progress so difficult on that concern?" The answers to this second question should start to elevate the process challenges.

▶ Ask yourself whether the same challenge is affecting two totally different situations. If the answer is yes, you have most likely identified a process challenge.

MAKE IT REAL

Q&A

I'm the secretary of our neighborhood association. Past experiences with this group haven't always been positive. How do I help people let go of the past, including disagreements, and focus on our new vision for the neighborhood?

- NEIGHBORHOOD NANCY

Dear Nancy,

Congratulations! You have identified a key process challenge: Helping "people let go of the past, including disagreements" is all about process.

Most people think the exercise of leadership in this situation is generating attention on the new vision for the neighborhood. But, given your insight, you know leadership requires letting people speak about past experiences. Review Chapter 17 in this book for specific ideas on speaking to loss.

Before you can tackle the content challenge (the new vision) you must put to rest the process challenges. You are thinking the right way.

Onward!

CHAPTER 3

DIAGNOSE SITUATION

Explore Tough Interpretations

As you work on your challenge, exploring tough interpretations becomes your crystal ball. This skill will help you anticipate the future and plan your leadership moves.

Humans tend to look at a situation and apply one easy or relatively comfortable explanation of what happened. To exercise leadership on adaptive challenges you'll need to train yourself to imagine multiple explanations — we call them "interpretations" — of the same information. And while we normally are glass-half-full kind of people, we realize it is important to recognize glass-half-empty situations to gain the right perspective.

"OOH, A BLINDFOLD – WHAT FUN!
BUT WHERE'S THE PIÑATA?"

HERE ARE SOME EXAMPLES OF WHAT WE MEAN.

First, we give you the "easy" interpretation, then several "tough" ones.
Either easy or tough could be right, or partially right. You'll be better equipped
to meet the future if you consider both.

> EASY INTERPRETATION: We lost the game because the refs cheated us.

> TOUGH INTERPRETATIONS: We lost because we didn't prepare enough.
> We lost because teammates don't trust each other. We lost because key
> teammates crack under pressure.

> EASY INTERPRETATION: To distinguish ourselves from the competition,
> we need a new strategic plan.

> TOUGH INTERPRETATIONS: What good is a new plan if our culture still
> stinks. We have tried but cannot execute a strategic plan. We don't like to
> focus on defined strategies and prefer the flexibility that comes with not
> really committing to anything.

> EASY INTERPRETATION: He is distant from his family because he
> prefers to do his own thing.

> TOUGH INTERPRETATIONS: He is suffering from mental illness. We've
> failed to be there for him in the past. Unacknowledged issues among family
> members keep him away.

> *As a species, we humans possess some unique capacities. We can stand apart from what's going on, think about it, question it, imagine it being different. We are also curious. We want to know "why?" We figure out "how?" We think about what's past, we dream forward to the future. We create what we want rather than just accept what is. So far, we're the only species we know that does this.*
> — MARGARET WHEATLEY

The exercise of leadership looks different based on the interpretation.

More interpretations mean more options. It's the difference between lodging a formal protest with the athletic conference and helping players develop mental strategies for handling stressful game situations. It's the difference between hiring a consultant to guide yet another strategic plan and exerting the will to carry out the current one. It's the difference between rarely seeing your loved one and gathering family members for a frank talk about your part of the mess.

The ability to explore uncomfortable explanations is a necessary leadership skill. If we don't explore tough interpretations, we see what's going on around us in simple, easy and benign ways. Then we apply technical strategies rather than adaptive approaches. Facing those difficult explanations allows us to imagine multiple ways forward and really understand what is required to make progress.

An interpretation is more than just an opinion. It's one explanation for why things are the way they are. Exploring tough interpretations is one aspect of diagnosing the situation. Diagnosing thoroughly helps you lead effectively.

WANT TO LEARN MORE ABOUT TOUGH INTERPRETATIONS?
Read the book "Immunity to Change" by Robert Kegan and Lisa Laskow Lahey.

How do you develop the skill?

Practice it. Imagine multiple explanations for a situation at work, at home or in the news. Recognize which interpretation might be easiest to "believe." Recognize it as just one way of looking at the situation. Practicing this skill is often easiest when you approach it as though you are renting the idea versus owning it. Exploring tough interpretations is about looking at a situation through every possible lens. Renting ideas gives you freedom to make tougher interpretations than you normally would.

TIPS FOR SUCCESS

▶ Base your interpretations on data you can observe, such as what someone said or did.

▶ When talking about tough interpretations with others, use language such as, "One interpretation might be ..." and "Another interpretation could be ..." That type of lead-in will help you and others remember those interpretations are just possibilities, not necessarily your opinion.

▶ Imagine four people: the rudest person you know; the most negative person you know; the bravest person you know; and the person you know who can most readily grasp a complex situation. Then ask yourself: What would each say about what's going on?

▶ Pretend this is happening to someone else in some other city, country or planet. Come up with interpretations from that vantage point.

If I had an hour to solve a problem, I'd spend 55 minutes thinking about the problem and five minutes thinking about solutions.

— *ALBERT EINSTEIN*

MAKE IT REAL
Q & A

I am a parent on the local school board. Lately we've had pretty big debates among teachers, parents and administration about the education our children are receiving. Our test scores keep going down. Parents blame the teachers, teachers blame the parents, and administrators blame lack of state funding. Everyone believes so firmly in his or her own thinking that I'm wondering how we can move forward?

- SAD FOR OUR SCHOOLS SELINA

Dear Selina,

What a frustrating situation! No one is trying to diagnose the situation. Everyone is set in his or her thinking. Leadership here is about getting the factions involved to consider multiple interpretations of what's happening.

You may be tempted to focus on solving the content problem. You might find yourself considering new reading and math programs, for example. Don't. Until you get the factions involved to consider uncomfortable interpretations, the right way forward will be elusive.

Try this. (1) Go first. Publicly acknowledge and "rent" explanations that put more of the blame on the school board. Be vulnerable and show others what it looks like to explore tough interpretations. (2) List different interpretations and share the list after you have five or six interpretations. Simply seeing a list of interpretations will ignite others' thinking.

Leadership here looks like helping the group better diagnose the situation. Good luck!

Onward!

P.S. Make sure the list you share with others always ends with: "Other interpretations?" Add others' ideas to the list.

CHAPTER 4

DIAGNOSE SITUATION

Take the Temperature

Good cooks know all about heat. Too much heat (too hot or for too long) ruins a meal — the stew turns to mush or the steak is too tough. But too little heat is disastrous too. Getting the oven hot enough and cooking just long enough are key to a perfect dish. Cooks benefit from recipes, thermostats, oven knobs and kitchen timers to help get it right.

Leadership requires similar attention to heat. You need enough energy around an issue to motivate people to do something differently. But too much heat can cause people to panic, fight, flee or shut down and ignore the situation. Knowing where people are on a scale of "cold" to "warm enough to do good work" to "things are so hot people are going nuts" is critical. It would be great if — like modern-day chefs — you had a digital readout telling you precisely how ready a group is to make progress.

Absent a digital readout, you need to examine the clues and make a diagnosis. It helps to know three common temperature indicators.

▶ ENGAGEMENT. How many people are working on the issue? The heat might be too low if there are just a few.

▶ PROGRESS. Is the conversation generating momentum or stagnation? Stagnation means not enough heat. Momentum equals heat.

▶ PURPOSE. Is there enough of a common purpose to keep people "checked in"? If the answer is no, there's not enough heat. If yes, there's plenty of heat.

It helps to be aware of what you might see if it's too hot or too cold.

FOR INSTANCE:

▶ People leaving the room either because they are bored or overwhelmed.

▶ Checking phones, falling asleep, zoning out of the conversation (again either bored or checking out because they can't handle the ambiguity or conflict).

▶ Body language that says people are either not interested (too cold) or angry and frustrated (too hot).

When doing adaptive work, taking the temperature is a full-time job. Don't let your system get too hot, but don't let things get so chilly people can avoid the work.

WANT TO LEARN MORE ABOUT TAKING THE TEMPERATURE?
Spend some time on the A.K. Rice Institute website at *akriceinstitute.org*. Purchase a book or attend one of the institute's events focused on understanding systems and group relations.

> *There are two different types of leaders. A person can either be like a thermometer or a thermostat. A thermometer will tell you what the temperature is. A thermostat will not only tell you what the temperature is, but it'll move you to the temperature you need to get to.*
>
> — *KEVIN MCCARTHY*

How do you take the temperature?

▶ ASK QUESTIONS AND LISTEN DEEPLY TO ANSWERS.
Provocative questions release the heat beneath the polite conversations by revealing diverse perspectives.

TRY THESE:

- What is on anyone's mind that you haven't said out loud yet?
- What values are in conflict here?
- What worries you?
- If there were an elephant in this room, what would it be?
- What are you most excited about here? Why?
- What's another way of looking at this situation?
- How might an outsider describe what is going on here?
- What would an outsider see that we are missing?
- Are we being as productive as possible here?
- On a scale of 1-10, how would you rate our level of productivity in the last 30 minutes?
- How will we take productivity up to a 10 for our remaining time?

▶ NOTICE BODY LANGUAGE. Name what you see (e.g., "No one is looking others in the eye.") and ask about the energy or emotion behind what bodies are doing.

▶ OBSERVE TONE OF VOICE. Is the tone open and exploratory (right amount of heat) or conflicted and reactive (too hot) or apathetic (too cold)?

▶ PROVIDE A PROVOCATIVE INTERPRETATION. If people ignore a difficult interpretation, you might have hit a hidden hot spot.

▶ MODEL THE TEMPERATURE YOU HOPE TO CREATE. Give people permission to be vulnerable, passionate or impatient with the rate of change by modeling those qualities yourself. Get hot yourself, and invite others to do the same. If no one follows your example, it may be a sign people don't share your enthusiasm for the issue.

▶ RECOGNIZE THE OUTSIDE FACTORS THAT MAY BE AT PLAY. People bring a lot of baggage that cannot be observed (e.g., a recent argument with a spouse or co-worker, getting ready for their child's soccer game, good or bad experiences with others in the room, etc.), which affects the temperature of the room.

Effectively taking the temperature allows you to intervene more skillfully to make progress. You'll be wiser and safer. You'll lower the risk level, because your efforts will be smarter and better timed. You'll know whether your first moves are to raise the heat or to work with the heat that's already there.

MAKE IT REAL
Q & A

I just became pastor of a church where the previous pastor had been in the position for more than 20 years. He was well liked but didn't challenge people. He let them do whatever they wanted as long as they didn't rock the boat. How can I start making changes among a pretty complacent group without getting thrown out right after starting?

- PASTOR PAUL

Dear Paul,

You'll find a lot of answers to what you need to do in the Energize Others and Intervene Skillfully sections of this book. However, make sure you take the temperature often!

"Making changes among a pretty complacent group" means you'll be raising the heat. Good for you! But it's a tenuous thing. Raise it too fast or too high and you'll blow the lid. Our advice is to create a small, diverse and informal group of congregation members to meet with regularly. The stated purpose would be an informal advisory board for you, the new pastor. However, you should also think of the group as a thermostat for the church.

Do more than just listen to them. Watch for clues about the temperature. For example, having trouble getting members to come to the meetings could mean the church's overall heat is too low — it just doesn't seem important to them. Or the heat might be just about right if a meeting runs long because of robust discussion and debate.

Onward!

P.S. The well-liked former pastor also might be an interesting gauge of the heat. So cultivate a relationship with him too.

CHAPTER 5

DIAGNOSE SITUATION

Identify Who Needs to Do the Work

A national fraternity with more than 100 years of history on more than 100 college campuses is facing a major cultural dilemma. Too many undergraduate brothers fail to live the fraternity's values and their actions threaten the long-term viability of the fraternity. The organization has grown from a network of college students into an international organization with a multimillion-dollar budget and more than 40 full-time employees. Without even realizing it, staff members can easily frame discussion about this challenge from their perspective. "What new policies do we need to implement?" "Should we hire more staff to focus on the problem chapters?" "Do we need to build stronger relationships with the undergraduates?" "Should we hold a listening session at the national convention to inform our discussions on this matter?"

Who needs to do the work?

As you attempt to understand this aspect of your own situation, sometimes the biggest realization is that who needs to do the work isn't you, or isn't just you, or isn't primarily you. Remember the principle: Leadership starts with you and must engage others. This is where the rubber of that principle hits the road.

Leadership on adaptive challenges is less about implementing solutions and more about creating the conditions for those with the problem to solve the problem.

Leadership is mobilizing others to make progress on daunting challenges. It's not a group project where one or two smart and organized people take on all the work while others happily defer. When doing adaptive work, the people with the problem have to solve the problem.

Technical work is different and can be done by experts and authorities.

EXAMPLES OF TECHNICAL CHALLENGES:

▶ The electrical grid goes down due to an ice storm. Who must do the work? The power company.

▶ A company's database is cumbersome and disorganized due to rapid growth. Who must do the work? A database specialist.

Stakeholders must do adaptive work. You can't do the work for them, but you can help them take up the work.

EXAMPLES OF ADAPTIVE CHALLENGES:

▶ A university president wants to create a culture of excellence throughout the university. Who must do the work? The president plays a role but needs deans, professors, administrators and staff to all work on a challenge as nebulous as "culture."

▶ A middle manager in the marketing department realizes the company's products aren't living up to their claims. Who must do the work? The manager is involved but a whole lot of others need to be involved too — product designers, senior managers, etc.

▶ A student wants to see less violence and bullying in her school. Who must do the work? The student can become a loud voice, but she is only one. Other students, teachers, administrators and parents must be engaged to make a lasting impact.

▶ A mother longs for her grown children to be more involved in each other's lives. Who must do the work? There is a limit to what the mother can do. Eventually the children themselves will need to "do the work."

The leadership in these examples is identifying and mobilizing others to take up the work and make it their own. It's a leadership failure if the only one believing in and working on the idea is the university president, middle manager, student or mother.

But who are these elusive "others"? A big part of exercising leadership is being able to answer this question for each adaptive challenge you face. Your answer will have a huge bearing on how you exercise leadership. Note that identifying who must do the work has a better chance of taking hold if you determine this as a group.

WANT TO LEARN MORE ABOUT WHO NEEDS TO DO THE WORK?
Read and use "The Collaborative Leadership Fieldbook" by David Chrislip.

How do you identify who must do the work?

▶ MAKE A LIST OF ALL THE FACTIONS INVOLVED WITH YOUR ISSUE.
On a scale of 1 to 10, rate each faction on how critical its support and help
is for success. Those scoring high are who must do the work. You may find
as you learn more and try new things that you will add or remove people
along the way.

▶ If making an exhaustive list sounds overwhelming, you might just START
WITH A SMALL LIST OF THE MOST IMPORTANT PEOPLE FOR THE
WORK. And remember, "most important people" means not just the people
you typically engage with but those most necessary for the work to progress.
People who are annoying or difficult to work with may be just the people
you need to move forward.

▶ CREATE TWO COLUMNS AND LIST PEOPLE YOU NORMALLY INVITE
TO BE INVOLVED IN THE FIRST COLUMN AND THOSE YOU HAVE
NOT INVITED IN THE SECOND. For the people in column one ask
yourself this: Why have you invited them? Why might they care? Are
they the right people to do this work? For the people in column two ask
yourself this: Why have they not been invited? Why might they care?
Why might it be important to invite them? With those questions answered,
re-evaluate the two columns to determine who is actually needed.

Lessons from History

Renowned chimpanzee researcher Jane Goodall
founded the Jane Goodall Institute, a global
nonprofit that empowers people to make a
difference for all living things. Goodall spent
years studying what it would take to improve
global understanding and treatment for all
living things. Much of her diagnosis focused
on research, public education and advocacy.
Ultimately, Goodall realized that to truly be
effective, she must mobilize others around the
globe to help. That led her "to identify who needs
to do the work" by creating a worldwide network
of young people who cared deeply for the
human community, for all animals and for the
environment, and who would take responsible
action to care for them.

How do you know you identified the right people?

- People start to talk about the issue as "our issue."
- Momentum is building. Experiments lead to progress and increased energy.
- Everyone loses (and wins in the end). Stakeholders are willing to let go of something they value for the sake of the common good.
- Diverse opinions are being shared. No groupthink.
- People agree that no important individuals or groups are being excluded.

Why is this important?

Identifying who needs to do the work is important because you'll need to tailor your leadership efforts accordingly, shifting from doing the work yourself to mobilizing others.

Often the biggest realization is simply that

"who"

needs to do the work isn't you, or isn't just you, or isn't primarily you.

MAKE IT REAL
Q & A

I recently completed my term as president of a fairly new organization. I know everything that needs to be done and how to do it to keep the group moving forward — you know, keep all the trains on schedule — so the group keeps coming to me for help. I enjoy being needed, but is my ongoing involvement in this way really what's best for the organization?

- **PRESIDENT PATRICE**

Dear Patrice,

No. Leave the work of running the organization to the new president. Everyone is replaceable. They'll learn what they need to learn. Instead, use your position as past president to "get up on the balcony" — creating the distance necessary for a different, more reflective perspective — and diagnose the adaptive issues facing the organization.

Your comment about being needed shows self-awareness. Most people are oblivious to how their own needs or perspective influence their behavior.

Onward!

CHAPTER 6

DIAGNOSE SITUATION

Test Multiple Interpretations and Points of View

We've found that too often, people (ourselves included) are satisfied with their first good idea. But exercising leadership requires us to generate numerous ways to understand an issue and multiple paths forward. We need to "try on" different ideas. Our friend and mentor Marty Linsky likes to encourage people to "just rent the idea ... you don't have to buy it ... just rent it."

Experience tells us that your ability to "rent" as many different ideas about what's going on in your situation will directly affect your ability to exercise leadership in that situation.

This idea of "testing multiple interpretations and points of view" is a key diagnostic activity. Here's a way of thinking of it that may be illustrative.

Imagine your car has been acting weird. It's making funny noises, not always starting, emitting strange fumes, etc. You take it to the mechanic. He opens the hood (point of view 1) and looks around. Next, he puts it on the lift so he can look underneath (point of view 2). Finally, he takes it for a spin (point of view 3). He briefly gives you his initial analysis: "Sir, it looks to me like there

"NEXT!"

are at least three possibilities. First, your timing belt is about to snap (interpretation 1). Or buildup on the engine block is clogging the exhaust manifolds (interpretation 2). Or you've never changed the oil and the car has 119,000 miles on it (interpretation 3).

The mechanic's next step would be to actually "test" those interpretations with specific diagnostic activity.

Let's start with the easier of the two: testing points of view.

Leadership challenges have multiple stakeholders with multiple points of view. How do senior managers see the challenge compared to frontline staff? How does the situation look if you are a newly elected official instead of a seasoned veteran? How about men compared to women? You get the idea.

Testing multiple points of view means taking deliberate steps to learn about their perspectives.

HOW DO YOU DO THIS?

▶ IDENTIFY THE FACTIONS INVOLVED.

▶ ENGAGE EACH FACTION, ESPECIALLY THOSE WHOSE SUPPORT YOU NEED THE MOST BUT CURRENTLY HAVE THE LEAST. Even engage your opposition. They may never come completely along, but you'll have a better chance of finding common ground if you look at the ground from their perspective.

▶ MEET WITH THEM, NOT TO CONVINCE THEM OF ANYTHING, BUT JUST TO LISTEN. Don't listen to reply. Listen to understand.

Testing interpretations can be trickier.

Let's go back to the mechanic example. There are three interpretations for why the car is acting up. Each requires a different fix. Based on the mechanic's knowledge and experience, all three could be the cause. He must run additional tests to determine which direction to head.

HERE'S A LEADERSHIP EXAMPLE.

The leadership challenge facing a small-business owner is how to mobilize employees to turn around sales. It's been more than a year since they were doing really well. She starts by considering multiple points of view. First, she looks to her own perspective (point of view 1). Second, she puts herself in the shoes of her sales team (point of view 2). Third, she explores what a customer might think (point of view 3). Finally, to flush out other possible interpretations, she contemplates the perspective of other employees (point of view 4).

Based on the multiple points of view, several interpretations come to mind for the owner. Her sales force just can't cut it (interpretation 1). The market no longer desires her products (interpretation 2). With the new shopping development on the outskirts of town, her location is no longer marquee enough to bring walk-in customers (interpretation 3), and she has been too distracted by a different business venture and hasn't provided the management her employees need (interpretation 4).

IN ORDER, TESTING THOSE INTERPRETATIONS WOULD LOOK LIKE THIS.

1.   Putting herself back in the sales role. Can she sell the product?

2.   Researching sales of similar products from other stores. Are their sales down too?

3.   Surveying the walk-in traffic she does get and surveying shoppers at the new development. Is this shopping area still attractive?

4.   Setting aside her other venture for a few months. Does my staff respond better when I'm more present?

HOW DO YOU TEST MULTIPLE INTERPRETATIONS?

▶   START BY IMAGINING MULTIPLE EXPLANATIONS (AKA INTERPRETATIONS) FOR THE ISSUE AT HAND. Review Chapter 3 to make sure you are exploring tough interpretations. Don't stop after your first good idea!

▶   JUST ASK OTHERS ABOUT THEIR THOUGHTS ON THE DIFFERENT INTERPRETATIONS. By offering multiple ideas, you'll help them explore new possibilities and enable them to give good feedback.

▶   RUN EXPERIMENTS. Remember, we experiment to learn, not to solve. Experiment to learn which interpretations seem most relevant. Review Chapter 23 on acting experimentally for more information.

MAKE IT REAL
Q & A

I have volunteered for a large nonprofit organization for many years. Lately, a lot of young people are getting involved just to pad their resumes instead of getting their hands dirty in the work. How do I get them to help out or get out?

- VOLUNTEER VICTOR

Dear Victor,

First, generate a few more interpretations. You have one so far, that they just want to pad their resumes. Start by just asking a few of them. Take them to breakfast and ask what's getting in the way of them being more engaged. Our guess is they will mention things you haven't thought about. Maybe additional interpretations will emerge, such as long-time volunteers spurning their ideas or that available volunteer times conflict too much with activities of their young families.

Next, test those interpretations. Ask people about them. Think about which seems most likely. Hold them all to be possible truths. Develop small interventions to try to make progress on each of them. See the Intervene Skillfully section for more ideas.

Onward!

Sometimes, the greatest obstacle to progress is our own ego. The need to be right or control everything blinds us to the realities of the situation. Or the fear of being disliked undermines our courage to act. We are afraid to move beyond the status quo. Anger, uncertainty or our personal baggage hampers our ability to assess and respond.

Self-awareness and a willingness to do things differently are at the core of this competency. Those two qualities are key to making progress. Because humans hate change. The way things are, no matter how crazy, is better than facing the unknown. Manage Self is a leadership competency, because progress requires taking risks and stepping outside your comfort zone for the sake of something you care about.

PART 2

MANAGE
SELF

CHAPTER 7

MANAGE SELF

Know Your Strengths, Vulnerabilities and Triggers

In Shakespeare's "Hamlet" Polonius says, "This above all: to thine own self be true, and it must follow, as the night the day, thou canst not then be false to any man." Our idea of "know your strengths, vulnerabilities and triggers" is a modern version of that classic advice.

A big part of exercising leadership is understanding and appreciating our humanness. People often assume they understand their strengths, vulnerabilities and triggers. But we tend to look at ourselves last. Rather than focus on our vulnerabilities, we point out the vulnerabilities in others. Rather than attempt to control our triggers, we note every time others are triggered. Rather than appreciate our strengths, we're envious of the strengths of others.

By knowing your strengths, vulnerabilities and triggers, you have a better chance of controlling them and of being intentional about how they can help — or hinder — you when exercising leadership.

LET'S DEFINE WHAT WE MEAN BY STRENGTHS, VULNERABILITIES AND TRIGGERS.

Strengths, in our context, are those leadership competencies and behaviors that come most naturally to you. We aren't talking just about your personality and career strengths (i.e. humorous, good public speaker, knowledge of a certain computer program, excellent project manager, etc.). We are more interested in getting you to know your leadership-related strengths for:

* Handling conflict
* Speaking from the heart
* Working across factions
* Inspiring a collective purpose
* Understanding the process challenges
* Etc.

Knowing which leadership dimensions come more naturally to you helps you pick experiments more likely to lead to success.

Don't shy from developing additional strengths, but be sure to leverage the ones you have.

Now let's talk about **vulnerabilities.** Notice we used the word "vulnerabilities" rather than "weaknesses." Vulnerabilities are different. Weaknesses are skills you could work to improve, such things as writing skills, time management or knowledge of a subject.

Vulnerabilities exist at a gut level. "Vulnerability" comes from a Latin word that means "a wound." Vulnerabilities encompass areas that make you open to attack — secrets, difficult relationships, past mistakes, private ambitions or personal cravings that could limit your ability to make progress on your leadership challenge. It's human nature to hide these vulnerabilities, even from ourselves. We expend tremendous energy trying to conceal our vulnerabilities and — if and when they are uncovered — to mitigate, dismiss or minimize them. Here are examples of vulnerability in action.

▶ A company's board of directors is losing faith in its longtime CEO. She rose through the ranks and made her mark as the champion for a once innovative product that no longer sells well. Her connection to that product could cause vulnerability for her. She might be unwilling to make tough choices about it because of what the product represents to her career.

▶ A legislator's ego and passion lead him to be more out front on a bill he supports but his district overwhelmingly opposes. His ego and passion become vulnerabilities in this situation.

▶ A young professional craves acceptance by the more established professionals in her company. She becomes more concerned with how she is perceived by others than whether her work is leading to the outcomes both she and the company desire. Her desire for acceptance is a vulnerability.

> *A wiser path may be to lean into our vulnerabilities, acknowledging them and embracing them.*

WANT TO LEARN MORE ABOUT YOUR
STRENGTHS, VULNERABILITIES AND TRIGGERS?

Participate in a Myers-Briggs Type Indicator assessment.

Read "Type Talk: The 16 Personality Types That Determine How We Live, Love, and Work" by Otto Kroeger and Janet Thuesen.

Don't be ashamed of your vulnerabilities. Acknowledging them (even if only to yourself) can lead to better decisions and better leadership. Understanding her connection to the product might lead the CEO to appoint a vice-president to make the final decisions about the product's future. The legislator might conduct a survey to check his passion against the district's interests. The young professional might get a coach to help keep her desire for acceptance in check.

Triggers are actions, behaviors, events or ideas that simply set you off — negatively or positively — and cause you to react more out of emotion than out of strategy. For example, one of your triggers might be a certain individual speaking up in a staff meeting, a comment your spouse makes from time to time, or the fact that you were or weren't invited to a certain meeting. We all have triggers, and it's hard to lead if we can't manage them.

Mindfulness helps us manage our triggers and responses. By increasing awareness of your triggers you create a "buffer zone" between the trigger (or impulse) and your reaction.

It is hard to do adaptive work, to learn, to be open to new ideas and to explore multiple ways forward. This is made harder when you act without thinking. Inability to control your triggers is a surefire way to fail in exercising leadership.

Between stimulus and response there is a space.
In that space is our power to choose our response.
In our response lies our growth and our freedom.
— VIKTOR E. FRANKL

TIPS TO MANAGE TRIGGERS

- Recognize when you've been triggered and count to 10 before responding.
- Think about what triggers you before heading into a meeting where you know it will happen. Make a plan to handle it.
- Have a totem or object you can look at when you're triggered to remind you of how you really want to behave.
- If a particular person triggers you, adopt a perspective that pushes against the feelings that set you off. For example: "This person really cares about this work and his passion comes through when he speaks." This might help you hold a different point of view when your normal reaction would be: "He is trying to derail this conversation!"

HOW CAN I BE MORE AWARE OF MY STRENGTHS, VULNERABILITIES AND TRIGGERS?

- Engage a leadership coach.
- Ask those who know you best what they think your strengths, vulnerabilities and triggers are.
- Debrief after a meeting with someone you trust. Ask questions such as, "In that situation, in what ways did I seem vulnerable?"
- Set aside time to reflect. Be honest with yourself.
- Think about how you normally respond to a trigger. What do you normally do? How do you respond?

> *A human being has so many skins inside, covering the depths of the heart. We know so many things, but we don't know ourselves! Why, thirty or forty skins or hides, as thick and hard as an ox's or bear's, cover the soul. Go into your own ground and learn to know yourself there.*
>
> — *MEISTER ECKHART*

MAKE IT REAL
Q&A

I try to be an involved citizen, but every time I attend a community meeting the people get me so frustrated. Several times I have just walked out! I really care about my community, so what do I need to do so I can be more engaged?

- SAMUEL, A CITIZEN WHO CARES

Dear Samuel,

How much do you really care? By walking out of the meeting — by not controlling your triggers — you are choosing your own comfort over helping your community. Here are two approaches to consider.

First, be a grownup. Don't collect your toys and go home. Life is full of people and situations you don't like. Those who lead learn how to hang in there anyway, because they care more about the issue than their own comfort. Suck it up, and stay in the meeting.

Second, find another way to engage. Community meetings are important, but our experience is you'll have far more impact if you build relationships with local officials. Ask them to coffee, learn their interests and help them understand your perspective. Leadership is about relationships. Build them.

Good luck! And remember, your community needs your involvement, but as a thoughtful, relationship-building citizen, not as someone stomping out mad.

Onward!

CHAPTER 8

MANAGE SELF

Get Used to Uncertainty and Conflict

Buckle up. It's going to be a bumpy ride. The difficult challenges holding back your organization are full of uncertainty, change and conflict. Anyone can lead, anytime and anywhere, but if you can't handle the twists and turns, get outta the car.

Typically, we covet comfort and avoid conflict. We call this "Kansas nice." We've also heard it as "Minnesota nice," "Iowa nice" or "Southern nice." Maybe you can relate.

When a large group meets, everything is wonderful and fine. But afterward, out in the parking lot, people cluster in twos and threes, venting frustrations and saying what they really think.

Adaptive challenges live in people's hearts and stomachs. By their very nature, adaptive challenges lack ready-made solutions. Where you see a need for change, other people fear losing something they now have. Keep in mind,

it isn't change that's scary but the loss that goes with it. People get passionate about issues that affect them. Values come into play. In the midst of this kind of work, no one knows the outcome. As uncertainty rises, so does conflict.

If you care about the future of your organization or community, leadership requires facing uncertainty and conflict for the sake of making progress.

Adaptive challenges are all about learning, and learning isn't easy. When the stakes are high and unknowns outnumber knowns, people get uncomfortable. They do everything possible to settle things quickly and make the discomfort disappear.

> *The better you get at holding steady amid uncertainty and conflict, the more prepared you'll be to help people learn and achieve a shared purpose.*

Uncertainty and conflict are often pegged as bad things — if the group doesn't know where it is going something must be wrong. Our experience suggests that uncertainty and conflict are signs that adaptive work is at hand. Leadership means harnessing the discomfort by focusing attention on the underlying causes.

How do you handle uncertainty?

▶ **Stay grounded in your purpose.** Remember that the discomfort is worthwhile.

▶ **Treat every situation as an opportunity to learn.**

▶ **Acknowledge risks, and keep them at a level you can manage.**

▶ **Don't put a time stamp on progress.** Adaptive work always takes more time than you think it will.

▶ **Be smart about what you ask of others.** Ask enough but not too much.

▶ **Don't forget what you do know.** Use it as your compass to navigate uncertainty.

How do you handle conflict?

▶ **See it coming.** Know what sets you off and what might trigger others.

▶ **Don't take things personally.** Instead, focus on what's best for the organization.

▶ **Keep one hand on the thermostat and keep conflict productive, not inflammatory.**

▶ **Value productive conflict.** Learn to manage it instead of eliminating it.

▶ **Seek out mediation skills or read "Getting to Yes" by Roger Fisher and William L. Ury.**

▶ **Walk in someone else's shoes.** Try to see where others are coming from.

▶ **Focus on observations and avoid interpretations.** Observations are pieces of data that are indisputable. For example: "I've noticed the marketing department never attends meetings initiated by the sales department." Interpretations are simply a guess at what the observations mean. For example: "It's clear the marketing department doesn't value the sales people."

TIPS TO HELP YOU GET USED
TO UNCERTAINTY AND CONFLICT

▶ When something is on your mind, say it.

▶ If you usually try to keep everybody happy, resist that urge
to be the peacemaker.

▶ Come to people's defense only as a conscious choice.
Avoid a knee-jerk response to save them.

▶ If you feel yourself taking something personally, get on the balcony.
Force yourself to make concrete observations about what is going on.

▶ If you say a meeting will last one hour, end the meeting on time
whether there is resolution or not.

GARTH BROOKS sums it up with his
chorus from "Standing Outside the Fire."

"Life is not tried, it is merely survived
if you're standing outside the fire."

WANT TO LEARN MORE ABOUT GETTING
USED TO UNCERTAINTY AND CONFLICT?

Check out Ken Segall's book "Insanely Simple: The Obsession that Drives Apple's
Success." Chapter 1, Think Brutal, nails the value of conflict. Chapter 9, Think
Skeptic, highlights the value of uncertainty.

What happens if you don't get used to uncertainty and conflict? We all start moving
down a path that no one either wants to take or should be taking, all because we don't
want to speak up or disappoint someone else. Check out Jerry Harvey's "Abilene
Paradox" to explore further.

MAKE IT REAL
Q & A

I've been working on an issue with my church and am finding myself continually triggered by a key player, Samantha, who seems against progress. It causes quite a bit of stress and often derails me. How do I "push through" this conflict without going crazy?

- FAITHFULLY CRAZY CHRISSIE

Dear Chrissie,

Don't "push through." Instead, try to embrace the conflict. Don't add to it, but acknowledge and study it. Why is it there? Most likely, Samantha represents the views of many others. Rather than seeing her as a source of conflict, think of her as a faithful and helpful adversary, someone helping you understand a point of view different from your own.

Invite Samantha to coffee, breakfast or lunch once a month for the next six months. Go into each occasion with a stance of curiosity about her opinions and history. Ready yourself with sincere, appreciative questions (e.g., "What experiences have helped shape your faith the most?"). Avoid snide questions (e.g., "Why are you holding up progress? Why are you dividing us?").

The two of you may not be fast friends six months from now, but you will know a lot more about where she is coming from, and that will help you handle the conflict.

Onward!

P.S. Don't forget that "love thy enemy" stuff your church preaches!

CHAPTER 9

MANAGE SELF

Choose Among Competing Values

Leadership is a clash of values. Not just between what you value and what I value. Leadership is a clash of your own values. Leadership is about elevating one thing we care about over something else we also value.

**What are values? And what does
it look like when they compete?**

Ask someone their values, and they will likely say such things as: family, faith, community, freedom, achievement, courage, hope, education, loyalty and love. These values are personal and bring positive feelings. Walk into a company and you might see their corporate values on the wall. Things such as teamwork, customer satisfaction, innovation, etc. Personally and professionally, these feel-good, positive ideas get named "core values." But simply proclaiming core values does not make them so.

Your actual
core values
*are revealed
in your behavior.*

FOR EXAMPLE:

▶ An organization that lists "innovation" as a core value but doesn't do anything to encourage new ideas values innovation in name only.

▶ The founder of a technology company who says he values creativity and input, but his lack of support for projects initiated by designers other than himself, and his inability to share airtime at staff meetings, tells a different story.

A real clue is what gets corporate support. For instance, does the sales staff always get the best training and perks? If so, the organization clearly values sales over other things. If you want to figure out what you value, look at your calendar, your checkbook and the people you spend time with. The same is true for a company, organization or community.

As you attempt to make progress on your challenge, you may need to negotiate a clash of values.

WANT TO LEARN MORE ABOUT
CHOOSING AMONG COMPETING VALUES?
Watch the movie or musical "Les Miserables."
Pay close attention to the value conflicts Marius
considers in the songs "A Heart Full of Love,"
"One Day More" and "Empty Chairs and Empty Tables."

HERE ARE EXAMPLES OF WHAT THAT NEGOTIATION LOOKS LIKE.

▶ A corporate team hasn't met its goals for the year. The organization values both accountability and harmony. The performances of a few members are holding the team back. Raising that issue and mobilizing people to address it will generate conflict. *Leadership in this situation means choosing accountability over harmony.*

▶ A middle manager's unit is stuck in a rut. The manager values everyone playing by the same set of rules but also values creativity and ingenuity. One of her subordinates is a creative genius but stretches the manager's patience by bending rules and norms. The subordinate comes in late and leaves the office for a coffee shop, claiming she works better there than in a cube. *Leadership in this situation may be about choosing creativity over rules.*

▶ A college student is struggling to find a job after graduation. Her father feels he needs to help by calling colleagues and friends and lining up interviews. But he also values her independence and ability to make her own way. *Leadership here might mean choosing to value independence over employment.*

How will you lead if you avoid conflict instead of raise the heat?

How will you lead if you avoid blame instead of explore tough interpretations?

How will you lead if you don't do anything that could fail instead of act experimentally?

Get Off Autopilot and Choose

Once, during a seminar, a man told Ed he cared about what his colleagues were discussing (they had been talking about the company's biggest challenges) but he was swamped and just didn't have time to work on those issues. Ed's response: "We have all the time in the world for the things we value most. It looks like you really don't value those things your colleagues are talking about. You would find time to work on them if you did."

Lessons from History

Chinese university students, at significant personal risk, organized pro-democracy demonstrations in Tiananmen Square in 1989. They occupied the square for seven weeks, peacefully protesting the authoritarian practices of the Chinese Communist Party and demanding reform.

As the days went on, most believed it was only a matter of time before the Chinese military would end the demonstration. Martial law was eventually declared and thousands of troops mobilized. All media were removed as troops began to roll into the square. An exact death toll is not known, but it is believed several hundred students were killed.

Chinese students faced brutality and death, choosing to elevate democracy and civil rights over personal safety.

The man was taken aback. He wasn't consciously choosing to not make progress on those important challenges. Rather, he was on autopilot. Choosing among competing values is the opposite of autopilot. It's one reason leadership is so rare.

Consciously choosing one value over another doesn't necessarily feel good. But it is necessary if you want to mobilize others to tackle tough challenges. Exercising leadership requires a level of awareness — some call it "mindfulness" — not typical of the average person. But you can develop this awareness through practice.

The bottom line is this: You are in charge of your own values and can influence the organization's values. But this only happens if you are aware of what they really are. Get off autopilot and lead.

How can we be more conscious of the values informing our choices?

▶ **Reflect in writing.** Explore the values underlying our behaviors and actions.

▶ **Ask yourself, "Why do I think I did what I just did? What value was behind it?"** For example, if you just curtly ended a conversation with a colleague, was it because you (1) value another project more, (2) don't ever value that person's contributions, or (3) are stressed about something else in your life.

▶ **For 10 days, log how you spend your time.** Record hours spent sleeping, working on different projects, enjoying family, exercising, etc. Then ask a friend or colleague to look at it and, just based on the data in the log, articulate what you value.

▶ **Ask someone who works with you regularly to list your values (good, bad and indifferent) based on the way you interact with others.**

How do we choose among competing values when exercising leadership?

▶ **Consciously!** Choose which values to elevate and which to sacrifice.

▶ **Articulate the values at play in a given leadership challenge.**
Then imagine what life would be like if you had to sacrifice one
or the other. Are the losses acceptable? Thoroughly imagining
the loss may make it easier to stomach.

▶ **Once in a while, accept that your values may be in conflict.**
Awareness is everything.

▶ **Embrace your contradictions.** Don't fool yourself. You value noble
things such as faith and family, yes. And your behavior suggests you
value other things too. Don't fight it. Don't judge.

MAKE IT REAL
Q&A

I really want to go far in my company. My assigned mentor tells me the way to do that is to "work hard, keep my head down and don't rock the boat." But the boat needs to be rocked. We aren't creating the best products, and I'm afraid sooner or later our customers will figure that out and go elsewhere. How do I "go far" and "rock the boat"?

- **WASHINGTON (A WANT-TO-BE BOAT-ROCKER)**

Dear Washington,

You seem to value your career prospects on one hand and what's best for the customer and by extension the company on the other. Those values are in conflict. Recognizing that clash is the first step. You'll notice that one of the values is about you and the other is about something bigger than you. Human beings tend to elevate themselves over the greater whole.

Leadership happens when you do the opposite.

Our advice? Start small. Don't write a manifesto. Start testing all the assumptions embedded in the "keep your head down and don't rock the boat" mantra. Is it folklore or truth? Float a nonthreatening idea for improvement by your manager and gauge the reaction. Collect and, again in a nonthreatening way, share data that tell the story about the company's declining quality.

Those around you might think you are nuts. But our experience is that the one who has the best interest of the organization in mind — even over their own best interests — usually is rewarded in the long run.

Your company needs you to exercise leadership!

Onward!

P.S. Regarding the "work hard" part of your mentor's mantra: That sounds right as long as it is within reason. Read the Take Care of Yourself section of this book.

CHAPTER 10

MANAGE SELF

Know the Story Others Tell About You

Don't you wish you could be in the room when the cast members from "The Bachelor," "Survivor" or "The Real Housewives" watch the final produced version of their reality shows? It must be fascinating as they watch how they are portrayed. During the reunion shows — when cast members come back to reflect on the experience — they say such things as, "Well, that's just how the show portrayed me. It didn't show you this and that."

(Authors' note: It is our deepest hope that if you are reading this book 15 years after publication you don't have the foggiest idea about these so-called reality shows. We'd take that as a sign our society is heading in a good direction.)

In reality, we are all a lot like those cast members. We have one version of how we see ourselves, but that isn't necessarily the story our co-workers would tell. It's as if we all are starring in our own movie about ourselves. We write and view the movie in our head and, at the end, we give the main character — ourselves — a standing ovation. Now imagine you're just a character in someone else's show. He or she is the main actor, and you simply play a supporting role. Are you the villain or a member of the team? Too aloof? Too happy-go-lucky? A key ally? Dependable? Dispensable?

You'll lead more successfully if you can imagine the stories others tell about you.

HERE ARE SOME EXAMPLES OF PEOPLE
WHO HAVEN'T YET MASTERED THAT SKILL:

▶ A politician thinks he can relate to everyone on the political spectrum — that he is a bridge builder. But others view him skeptically as coming from an extreme point of view.

▶ A newly hired CEO thinks she is there to turn around the company based on her past success turning around other companies. But employees view her as a hatchet-wielding menace preparing to slash jobs.

▶ A teacher thinks of himself as a great educator. His students get top marks. The school district and his alma mater have recognized his teaching excellence. Rather than seeing him as a gifted teacher, some colleagues see him as a ladder climber who cares more about his resume than collaborating with other teachers.

From a leadership perspective, it's easy to see why knowing what others are saying and thinking is important. The politician, knowing not everyone sees him as a bridge builder, might work harder to engage divergent factions. The new CEO might engage her employees around their needs and desires, rather than assume they want a turnaround specialist. The teacher might focus more on learning from others in his building and nominate others for teaching awards.

WANT TO LEARN MORE ABOUT KNOWING
THE STORY OTHERS TELL ABOUT YOU?
Simply watch a few episodes of the show "The Office." You'll learn a lot about what this idea does not look like by watching the main character, Michael Scott. And remember, if you can't identify the Michael Scott in your office, then you are the Michael Scott!

Knowing how others perceive you — or being able to imagine how they might perceive you — helps you be more effective. You can better adapt to the situation and experiment more wisely.

So what do you do with these stories once you know them?

One thing is for sure. We are not saying you should go out and change everything about yourself. After all, this concept is called "know the story others tell about you" not "know the story others tell about you and change." By better knowing the stories others tell about you, you can better manage yourself and be more effective at exercising leadership.

So what happens if you hear something that resonates with you? For example, maybe you realize you're not articulate when speaking in front of groups. You clam up and start talking in circles, leaving everyone in the room thinking you're not only unprepared but incompetent. You can enhance these skills. You can join Toastmasters or take a public speaking class. In this case, it makes sense that once you know the story, you can take steps to rewrite it.

For a contrary example, let's say you hear that you expect too much and come across as competitive. Your colleagues feel like you are trying to be better than them. Deep down you know you're really passionate about the work and want to be part of something successful. In this case, you aren't willing to compromise in hopes that others will like you more. However, you might decide you need to do a better job communicating with colleagues about your passion and how much you care about them and what they bring to the table.

HOW DO YOU LEARN THE STORIES OTHERS TELL ABOUT YOU?

▶ DIRECT FEEDBACK ABOUT SPECIFIC SITUATIONS. Ask, "What could I do better in this situation? What's my part of this mess? If you could change one thing about me related to this situation, what would it be?"

▶ WATCH FOR INDIRECT FEEDBACK. Pay attention to body language and the song beneath their words. What are they not saying?

▶ USE YOUR IMAGINATION. Think of multiple ways someone could view you in the situation.

THINGS TO KEEP IN MIND WHEN SEEKING FEEDBACK

▶ GROUND YOUR INQUIRY IN A SITUATION. ("Sam, at the meeting on Thursday, how do you think I was perceived?")

▶ EMBED IN YOUR QUESTIONS THE ACKNOWLEDGMENT THAT YOU ARE IMPERFECT. ("I know I have lots of room for improvement. Maybe you can help. What I'm wondering is ...")

▶ GIVE THEM PERMISSION TO BE FRANK WITH YOU. ("I would really like your honest feedback ...")

▶ COMMUNICATE YOUR PURPOSE. ("This is important to me, because I'm trying to help move us forward on _____ and knowing how I'm perceived will help me.")

> *The same way that you are*
> *the main character of your story,*
> *you are only a secondary character*
> *in everybody else's story.*
>
> — *MIGUEL ANGEL RUIZ*

MAKE IT REAL

Q & A

I have been retired for three years. I served as the executive director of a well-known not-for-profit for 15 years. After spending some time away, I was asked to come back as a volunteer. I'm still passionate about the cause and have jumped back in to help. Some are welcoming me with open arms but others don't seem as friendly as they were before. Any advice?

- ELLIE THE EX-E.D.

Dear Ellie,

Here are just a few of the stories that could be swirling around in people's minds: You don't trust the new executive director. You aren't really passionate about the cause; you just can't stand retirement. The new executive director is struggling, and the board must have encouraged you to help.

Yours is a delicate situation. Ask others how you are perceived. (See the tips earlier in this section.) Don't ignore the unfriendly behavior. Assume that something is up, and try to get to the bottom of it.

Hang in there and let your passion for the not-for-profit's cause fuel you as you work through these difficulties.

Onward!

CHAPTER 11

MANAGE SELF

Experiment Beyond Your Comfort Zone

If you want to make progress on your challenge, you'll need to say yes to a little discomfort.

Successful entrepreneurs understand this instinctively. As soon as one idea or product is launched, they are thinking about the next one. They are constantly expanding their thinking, trying new things and building new skills. They regularly experiment beyond their comfort zone.

Your preferred way of working — your usual style — that's your comfort zone. You may have achieved a lot of success operating this way. Good for you. But chances are that if you want to make progress on a really big challenge — or if you want change to happen faster or last longer — you'll need to push beyond what's comfortable.

"YEAH, I GET THE PART ABOUT YOU
FEELING BETTER WITH TRAINING WHEELS
ON, BUT HERE'S THE THING..."

Marshall Goldsmith's book "What Got You Here Won't Get You There: How Successful People Become Even More Successful" hits on this idea.

Expand your comfort zone through low-risk experiments. When we experiment, we learn. Each time you stop to ask whether your normal approach — your comfort zone — is the correct one, you open yourself up to possibilities. You discover new options. You build the resilience required to lead.

This should be obvious, but experimenting beyond your comfort zone will mean you are uncomfortable. Our default is comfort. We crave it. Our lives revolve around routines. Leadership requires you to resist the human urge for comfort.

Your comfort zone is unique. Personality, culture, position and a whole bunch of other things factor into who we are and what we define as our "edge" — the place where we start experimenting. You don't need to do anything grand. It can be as small as asking a question when you would normally say nothing or staying quiet when you would usually speak up.

The important thing is that you choose to experiment, it is a conscious choice, and you learn something.

And while it sounds risky (and it is) you will likely think differently, engage differently and act differently, and then, hopefully, the outcome will look different.

WANT TO LEARN MORE ABOUT GETTING BEYOND YOUR COMFORT ZONE?
Read "What Got You Here Won't Get You There: How Successful People Become Even More Successful" by Marshall Goldsmith.

SO HOW DO YOU KNOW IF YOU'RE EXPERIMENTING?
ASK YOURSELF THREE QUESTIONS.

1.   Am I outside my comfort zone with this effort?

2.   Am I unsure of the exact outcome of each experiment?

3.   Am I learning?

If the answer is "no" to any of these, you probably aren't leading anyone to do adaptive work. You may be managing the status quo very effectively and that may be work, but it's not leadership.

INDICATORS YOU ARE SAFELY OUTSIDE YOUR COMFORT ZONE

▶   YOU ARE FEELING INCOMPETENT BUT WILLING. You may not see the next step, but you are willing to put your foot out.

▶   YOUR PULSE QUICKENS. You feel a healthy level of anxiety.

▶   YOU ARE TAKING CONSCIOUS ACTION. Experimentation is a choice, not a reaction.

INDICATORS YOU HAVE GONE TOO FAR

▶   YOU HAVE LOST YOUR IDENTITY. Make change in small increments, but not so much that you are no longer recognizable.

▶   YOU HAVE NO CLEAR PURPOSE. Don't go beyond your comfort zone just for the thrill. Know the reason behind your risk.

▶   YOU ENTER THE DANGER ZONE. If you are on the verge of being fired or quitting, find a safer approach.

▶   THE ANXIETY IS CONSUMING YOU. The anxiety should feel interesting and healthy, not destructive and consuming.

**SIMPLE WAYS TO PRACTICE
EXPERIMENTING BEYOND YOUR COMFORT ZONE
(GIVE ONE OR TWO A TRY IN THE NEXT WEEK)**

▶ Meet with someone in your company who makes you uncomfortable.

▶ Take a stand on something important to a colleague or a friend.
  (Or don't take a stand if taking a stand is the norm for you.)

▶ Be curious, and ask a question rather than jumping in to give advice.

▶ Don't assume you understand exactly what your colleague is talking
  about. Instead, ask a clarifying question such as, "What do you mean
  by that?" or "Please, can you tell me more?"

▶ If you typically work 50- or 60-hour weeks, work a 40-hour week,
  and pay attention to what happens as a result.

▶ If you normally weigh in early and often in meetings, try counting
  to 10 before talking.

▶ Invite yourself to a meeting on a topic you are curious about.

Lessons from History

It was 1939 and Nazi Germany and Britain had gone to war. The new king of England, George VI, suffered from a lifelong stammer. As popularized in the 2010 movie "The King's Speech," the king set aside his own discomfort with public speaking and stepped to the microphone to declare war on Germany. Millions around the world heard the radio address. It's hard to imagine a public figure more outside his comfort zone. King George VI delivered an inspiring speech that rallied the British people and set the tone for six long years of war.

Leadership rarely fits nicely within your everyday schedule. Leadership is about doing what is needed, not what is comfortable.

**Here are two poems to inspire you
to reach beyond your comfort zone.**

*It may be that when we no longer know what to do
we have come to our real work,
and that when we no longer know which way to go
we have come to our real journey.
The mind that is not baffled is not employed.
The impeded stream is the one that sings.*

— WENDELL BARRY, "THE REAL WORK"

*We never know how high we are
Till we are called to rise;
And then, if we are true to plan,
Our statures touch the skies.
The heroism we recite
Would be a daily thing,
Did not ourselves the cubits warp
For fear to be a king.*

— EMILY DICKINSON

As a longtime local county commissioner, I've always been partial to the way we've engaged in politics. You know, taking phone calls, attending community gatherings and personal letters to constituents. Unfortunately, we're just not getting a lot of feedback this year, and we really need some guidance from community members. How can we hear from more people?

- FRANK THE FAITHFUL PUBLIC SERVANT

Dear Frank,

Times they are a changing, Frank! Yard signs, letters, calls and town hall meetings no longer keep constituents engaged. Does this mean you need to start tweeting, podcasting and hosting webinars? No. But the ineffectiveness of your traditional methods shows you need to do something different.

We admire your desire for feedback from constituents. But what do you value most? Is it hearing from your constituents or staying within your comfort zone with the traditional ways you mentioned? You seem like a guy who is choosing the latter.

Rather than "take phone calls," make 10 phone calls a day to randomly selected constituents. You'll learn a lot and they'll be stunned. Find a young up-and-coming politician — the one with the huge campaign following who volunteers everywhere and constantly makes waves. Whether you agree with his or her politics or not, take that person to breakfast and ask for advice. He'll be flattered, and you'll learn new approaches.

Want to put some pressure on yourself to experiment? Tell your local paper you want to have 1,000 conversations with constituents in the next year and ask them to hold you to it!

Good luck and thank you for your service!

Onward!

CHAPTER 12

MANAGE SELF

Take Care of Yourself

Countless pressures drive today's worker (you) toward burnout. Stress may even be damaging your health. We all experience the competing pulls of work, community involvement, family and friends. We know how difficult it can be to attend to your own health and well-being.

But, if you want to respond effectively to the demands of work and community, you need to be at your best: healthy, focused and flexible. If you get sick, lose your passion for the work or make a bad decision when sleep-deprived, everybody loses.

We know from our own experience you can't lead effectively if you are exhausted and irritable. So, we challenge you to imagine how you will take better care of yourself—physically, emotionally, intellectually and spiritually. Remember, it's for your own sake and for the good of all who look to you for inspiration.

During his first job after college, Ed remarked to his colleagues that what they needed was a little time to sit in a beanbag and read Life magazine. Enough with the constant movement, crazy schedules, hurried pace. They all needed time to think, distill and rest so they could be at their creative best. To this day, his early colleagues poke fun at Ed for his "beanbag and Life magazine speech." He was getting at what we now call "take care of yourself," one of the key ideas under the leadership competency Manage Self. It is all about being at your physical, mental, emotional and spiritual best so you can best exercise leadership and make an impact.

Leadership is risky. When trying to get others to take on difficult challenges, you need your wits, creativity and energy. We've all been stressed out. Maybe you are up to your eyeballs right now. When stress happens your quality of work plummets. Relationships are strained. Health suffers. Your ability to rally anyone to do anything outside the norm (e.g., to exercise leadership) is dramatically diminished.

These days, Ed makes it clear that KLC wants employees who are "fully- whelmed," not overwhelmed and not underwhelmed. The expectation is that team members work a "hard, efficient and fun 40" hours each week.

A "take care of yourself" culture helps organizations thrive too!

Key to our thinking about the "hard, efficient and fun 40" is that embracing it promotes important decisions and innovation. People are forced to prioritize ("Of all the things I could do, what should I do?"). Equally important, the "hard, efficient and fun 40" stimulates innovation that probably would not have occurred otherwise. People find new ways to get things done when time is limited.

Take care of your body.
It's the only place you have to live.

— *JIM ROHN*

HERE IS A MEMO FROM ED TO HIS TEAM.

Several times over the years, staff has heard me describe my aspiration that they are not overwhelmed or underwhelmed, but rather "fully-whelmed." We aren't interested in people coasting or being stressed out. I don't want our people working 60-, 70- or 80-hour weeks. While in some work environments that type of effort is rewarded and even expected, at KLC it is misguided. You won't be at your best working that much. I believe 40 hours of "your best you" is much better for KLC (and you!) than 60 hours of "stressed-out-you." In that spirit, let me be clear with the expectations from senior staff.

- **Hard, Efficient and Fun 40 hours.** We expect you to work a hard, efficient and fun 40 hours each week.

- **Family and Friends.** We value family and friendships and believe you are a better employee if you do too.

- **Sleep and Exercise.** We value sleep and exercise and believe you are a better employee if you do too.

- **Outside Interests.** We value being involved in civic life, faith communities and/or hobbies and believe you are a better employee if you do too.

Come talk to your supervisor or me if you are out of whack on one or more of the above. Also, speak up if you see senior staff or others sending mixed messages about those items.

Bottom line: KLC is a place that will allow you to create the best life possible for yourself. Why? Because we care about you and because KLC will be stronger if you are happy and healthy.

This is beyond work-life balance. This is about how to prepare yourself to lead. If we don't bring our best selves to our work, we're less likely to engage in leadership effectively.

Lessons from History

TAKE CARE OF YOURSELF

Prime Minister Winston Churchill read a novel every day during World War II. Recognizing that your challenges are not quite the same as defeating Nazi Germany, shouldn't you be able to find time to take care of yourself?

WHAT DOES TAKING CARE OF YOURSELF LOOK LIKE?

- Recognize when you need to care for yourself. See the need coming. Don't let yourself get overwhelmed.
- Find what renews you, such as personal projects, quiet time, physical activity, etc.
- Maintain compassion for yourself.
- Hold to your own purpose. Say "no" often.
- Get back to the basics:
  Stay home when you're sick.
  Use your vacation days.
  Eat well and exercise.

WHY DON'T WE TAKE CARE OF OURSELVES MORE?

- **Competing values.** We choose to make other commitments more important.

- **It's risky.** We fear job loss, income loss and the perception that we're selfish.

- **It's against the culture.** Caring for ourselves is not valued. (See the beanbag and Life magazine reference earlier in this chapter.)

WARNING SIGNS

- You are restless, irritable and discontent.
- You no longer have compassion for others. You don't have the patience to start where they are.
- You forget things.
- You become physically ill.
- You take things personally.
- You lose control of your triggers.
- You feel crazy busy with no real progress to show for it.

WHAT IS THE COST OF NOT TAKING CARE OF YOURSELF?

While only you can answer this question, at its core, the highest cost of not taking care of yourself is losing your ability to make a lasting impact on whatever matters most to you.

WANT TO LEARN MORE ABOUT TAKING CARE OF YOURSELF?

Check out "Crazy Busy" by Kevin DeYoung
and "Daring Greatly" by Brené Brown.

Watch Arianna Huffington's four-minute TEDWomen
Talk "How to Succeed: Get More Sleep."

MAKE IT REAL
Q&A

If you want to get ahead in my department you are expected to put in 60- to 70-hour weeks. Balance that with my family, church and volunteer obligations, and I know I'm approaching burnout. I've seen some of my friends crash, and I don't want to be them. What should I do?

- BURNED OUT TANISHA

Dear Tanisha,

Your question is about values. What do you value the most? Given the spirit of your question, working 60-70 hours each week in that environment suggests you value how you are perceived day to day by peers and managers more than you value exercising leadership.

Cut your hours back to 40-50. Expect criticism and snide remarks. Hold steady. Don't let it get to you. Channel your energy into discovering new ways to become more efficient. Share your experiment with others. I bet a few will join you. After a few months, one of two things will happen. You will either start a small revolution that will successfully lead to changing the culture of your department or you will discover it is time to find a new job.

Remember, if you want to lead, you must take care of yourself.

Onward!

P.S. Leadership is about taking the road less traveled. Those exercising leadership are usually NOT doing what "everyone" else in the organization, company or community is doing.

When it comes to adaptive challenges, progress takes more than getting people riled up. The competency of Energize Others is about more than motivation. Energize Others means engaging all the stakeholders — those with influence and those affected but less likely to have their voices heard. Success comes when all parties are engaged and working on the challenge.

Energizing the full range of stakeholders for a common purpose is difficult. It takes commitment, experimentation and a willingness to take risks. It's slow work engaging people on their terms, creating a process everyone can trust. Nevertheless, it's worth the effort if the experiments bring progress.

PART 3

ENERGIZE OTHERS

CHAPTER 13

ENERGIZE OTHERS

Engage Unusual Voices

This is a rule: Engage unusual voices.

You may think you can save the day and make the daunting challenge disappear. It's tempting to think you can simply work with those you already know, ones "with" you on whatever challenge you undertake. But leadership on the kind of challenge you've identified just doesn't work that way. Making progress on entrenched — once again, adaptive — challenges means thinking outside the box.

We are not big on rules. But we do have at least one: Engage unusual voices. If you are facing an adaptive challenge, do not violate this rule.

Usual voices are your go-to crew: the people in your department, your most trusted volunteer board member or the colleague from another department who thinks like you. Unusual voices are just that — the people and groups that you seldom engage. They have a stake in the issue but their opinions are rarely sought. They are outside your immediate circle but have the influence you'll need to produce change.

[handwritten annotations: Kids!, church groups, Local Business owners —, Chambers, unusual voices for me Commissioner, our Boards, MCSSN members]

For a senior executive, usual voices might be other senior executives, the board and friends, and colleagues from similar organizations. Unusual voices might be frontline employees or clients.

For a middle manager, an unusual voice — and exactly the person you need on your side — could be that senior executive. The executive may be the only one who can speak on behalf of the frontline people who report directly to you and are in touch with customers day in, day out.

For a neighborhood volunteer, the usual voices might be neighbors and family members. The unusual voices might be people at city hall and business owners.

Ed's son Jack came to him one day with ideas for a new playground at school. His classmates (Jack's usual voices) had been bantering about the subject for a few days. They agreed that something should be done and that they deserved an awesome playground. But progress wouldn't be made, Ed explained to Jack, unless Jack and his schoolmates engaged the voices that would be harder and less obvious for them to work with. The unusual voices in Jack's situation were teachers, administrators and parents.

Leadership on tough challenges (and getting a new playground counts as a tough challenge for 8-year-olds!) requires engaging both usual and unusual voices.

Why is it important to engage unusual voices?

True progress isn't made without them, because people whose voices aren't usually heard see important things others don't (e.g., the senior executive is detached from the experience of the customer, but the frontline employee deeply gets it) or because some of the work actually belongs to them (e.g., the schoolkids alone can't build a new playground).

In these troubled, uncertain times, we don't need more command and control; we need better means to engage everyone's intelligence in solving challenges and crises as they arrive.

— MARGARET J. WHEATLEY

There are plenty of good reasons not to engage unusual voices. It's risky. You might be rejected. It takes time. It's outside your normal box (comfort zone). Your assumptions about what some people are capable of (or might care about) get in the way. But it's a rule: Engage unusual voices.

HOW TO GET STARTED ENGAGING UNUSUAL VOICES?

▶ FIRST IDENTIFY YOUR USUAL VOICES. Don't disengage from them. Simply acknowledge them as your usual voices.

▶ IDENTIFY OTHER VOICES CONNECTED TO YOUR ISSUE. List everyone who will be affected by a cause or decision.

▶ MAKE IT SIMPLE. Meet with them over coffee or breakfast.

▶ DON'T TELL THEM YOU ARE RIGHT AND THEY ARE WRONG. Listen to them. Meet them where they are.

▶ ONLY AFTER WORKING HARD TO UNDERSTAND THEM, BEGIN ASKING FOR THEIR FEEDBACK ON YOUR OPINIONS.

WANT TO LEARN MORE ABOUT
ENGAGING UNUSUAL VOICES?

Check out Roz Lasker and John Guidry's book "Engaging the Community in Decision Making: Case Studies Tracking Participation, Voice and Influence." The book focuses on civic situations, but its themes are applicable across sectors.

MAKE IT REAL
Q&A

Every year near the holidays, our church has a community-wide dinner to support the needy. It takes a lot of resources, particularly people, to put this on. Our planning team, all members who have been involved from the start, really wants to get the younger people in our church to volunteer, but since they've never been involved, how do we do that?

- FA-LA-LA FELICIA

Dear Felicia,

The first step is recognizing that the group who you need to involve is not yet at the table. You might start by inviting younger church members to join your planning team. The important thing is to not just ask them to participate, but to truly give them a seat at the table and listen to what they say.

You might also prepare for what this might mean to your team. When you include voices that haven't been part of the process before, be ready for your own ideas and ways of doing things to be challenged. So make sure your purpose is clear and then open up your heart and mind to the possibilities that exist when you truly engage with unusual voices.

Onward!

CHAPTER 14

ENERGIZE OTHERS

Start Where They Are

Start where they are, not where you are.

As you exercise leadership, at some point you will be asking, compelling, cajoling or encouraging others to change. It's critical to know where those individuals and groups (aka factions) are coming from, their history and what they care about related to your leadership challenge. You can't lead others if you don't know where they stand.

Leadership is about mobilizing others. Mobilizing starts with curiosity and questions: What do these people care about? What's their perspective on the proposed change? What do they stand to gain or lose?

"THIS WAY!"

The challenge may appear differently based on where you are in the organization. A tough challenge looks a lot different depending on whether you are CEO, middle manager or on the front line.

It's a lot harder to hear, "I don't care what you have to do this afternoon, this project is important and you will focus on it first," than, "I know this team has a lot on its plate. We're all feeling the crunch of being short-staffed right now. With that said, it looks like we have a short deadline on this new project and we all need to do what we can to get it done by the end of the week."

Obviously, in the second example, the boss addresses feelings and concerns (the adaptive elements) right from the beginning. By acknowledging where they are as a team, the boss makes it more likely that they'll be successful in the long run.

Failing to start where they are leads to rebellion, stagnation and failure. Taking others' feelings and experience into account prepares you to manage the heat (see Diagnose Situation: Take the Temperature) and energy in the room, particularly if people won't like what you have to say.

HERE'S AN EXAMPLE FROM OUR ORGANIZATION.

▶ KLC is designed and built to influence and eventually transform the civic culture of our state. But we learned early on that few people wake up in the morning with that lofty idea on their to-do list. While "transforming the civic culture so it's more effective" may be our leadership challenge, it's not "where they (the vast numbers of people we interact with) are." We've learned people come to KLC for help with their leadership challenges, often about issues and dynamics in their organization. Once we understand their leadership challenge and provide resources and experiences that help them make more progress, we notice a willingness — even an excitement — about helping us with our leadership challenge.

HOW DO YOU START WHERE THEY ARE?

- **Ask questions.** What do they care about? What is their perspective? What is their history with this idea?

- **Just listen, not to reply but to understand.**

- **Explore every explanation for what is going on in the situation.**

WHAT GETS IN THE WAY OF "STARTING WHERE THEY ARE"?

- **We are blinded by our own vision.** Our vision is so obvious for us that we fail to realize others come to the same issue with vastly different history. If you find yourself trying to convince another person of the brilliance of your idea, you are probably not starting where they are.

- **Time and values.** In our rush to solve problems, we don't value engaging others, listening to them and trying to understand them. Even in our results-driven world, if the challenge is adaptive we will see better outcomes when we take others into account from the beginning.

- **We are misguided.** We jump to solving the problem rather than understanding the people involved and the true nature of the problem.

- **Lack of knowledge and empathy.** The less we know about others and their experiences, the less likely we are to understand their point of view.

HERE ARE TWO QUICK WAYS TO DETERMINE WHETHER YOU ARE STARTING WHERE THEY ARE.

- First, as you listen to the group's conversation, is the "main thing" staying the "main thing"? Failure to start where they are typically means groups get distracted by things that are more important to them.

- Second, observe whether all factions are connecting with the discussion rather than becoming defensive or contradictory. You've started where they are if ideas resonate with everyone.

> *To effectively communicate, we must realize that we are all different in the way we perceive the world and use this understanding as a guide to our communication with others.*
>
> — *ANTHONY ROBBINS*

MAKE IT REAL
Q & A

I'm a new vice-president in a midsize company. The company is successful, but I was brought in to help take it to the next level. I hit the ground running with a robust 90-day action plan. My challenge is that my ideas are meeting lots of resistance. How do I gain traction for my ideas?

- TRACTION THANH

Dear Thanh,

Shred your 90-day action plan. Recycle the scraps and replace it with a 90-day plan to engage and listen. You are the new guy. Coming in to implement a package of ideas isn't the way to go.

Your adaptive challenge is to help a group of already successful people reach the next level. Your job would be easier if the company wasn't successful. Then your colleagues might be desperate enough to grab on to any idea you, "the savior," had to offer. Your 90-day action plan is a threat to them. You are trying to get them to change without understanding what that change might mean to them. Engage them. Listen to them. Ask questions. Don't let your mind start developing ideas or solutions. Discern next steps only after you really understand where they are coming from.

Onward!

CHAPTER 15

ENERGIZE OTHERS

Work Across Factions

Working across factions happens when someone holding certain values and beliefs engages productively with another with different values and beliefs.

"Productively" is the key word.

The cable news channels are filled with talking heads from across the political spectrum. The pundits speak eloquently (maybe). They each are there to represent their faction (liberals, conservatives, libertarians, moderates, extremists, etc.). No one is there to work across factions. Their interaction is reduced to mini-speeches, given to each other and their audience. Each mini-speech has the goal of trying to convince others that the speaker's faction is right or, maybe even more likely, appealing to their own hard-liners and enforcing their already strongly held values and beliefs.

Exercising leadership on adaptive challenges involves working across factions, not simply trying to beat them into submission.

What are factions?

Factions are groups of people who share values. They are often loyal to the same things and share a common orientation to the work before them. Factions can be political (conservative, liberal, etc.), generational (boomers, Gen Xers, company founders, new hires, etc.), geographical (rural, urban, headquarters, field office, etc.), spiritual (religious, agnostic, atheist, etc.), personality driven (introverts, extraverts, etc.), organizational (board members, staff, departments, contractors, volunteers, etc.), among many more. Why is it critical to work across factions?

One faction ruling (the country or the office) with a 50.1 percent majority is fine for technical problems. Trying to solve adaptive challenges in the same manner is a recipe for stalemate. Adaptive challenges are about values and culture. You can't impose values and culture upon other factions. They need to be crafted together. When you help diverse factions find common ground, you are on your way to making progress for the long haul.

Working across factions is hard.

Working across factions requires more time "diagnosing the situation" than we like. Working across factions starts with doing lots of work to understand the perspective of the other factions. To work across factions you need to understand their loyalties, values and beliefs. You need to imagine the situation from their point of view and do so in an authentic and honest way.

How do we start?

Once you understand where the other faction is coming from, start looking for common ground. Go for the low-hanging fruit. Generate some good will and build from there. And don't be surprised if over time you find yourself in one faction for a certain project, and then in a new faction for another.

And brace yourself for tough discussions with your own faction. They might not want you consorting with the enemy. Expect questions like, "You did what? You met with whom? And you didn't even convince them they are wrong? Who the heck do you think you are?" It can be especially hard to work across factions if you hold an authority role among your faction (e.g., the Senate majority leader or the accounting department manager). Because you have been put in that role to advocate for certain things, your faction might not like you working with the others.

WANT TO LEARN MORE ABOUT
WORKING ACROSS FACTIONS?

Read "Team of Rivals," Doris Kearns Goodwin's brilliant
biography of Abraham Lincoln and his Cabinet.
Ask yourself, "How did Lincoln work across factions?"

TIPS FOR WORKING ACROSS FACTIONS

▶ FOCUS ON BUILDING TRUST FIRST. Invite someone to lunch. Don't make this too complicated.

▶ IDENTIFY OVERLAPPING INTERESTS AND BUILD OFF THEM, RATHER THAN FOCUSING ON DISAGREEMENTS.

▶ HAVE A MINDSET THAT YOU MIGHT NOT BE RIGHT. Be open to discovering new possibilities together.

▶ ACKNOWLEDGE LOSS THE OTHER FACTIONS MIGHT EXPERIENCE, RATHER THAN SUGARCOATING THE SITUATION.

▶ ASK QUESTIONS. Not loaded ones such as, "Don't you think the company will crumble if your ideas get implemented?" But sincere, open-ended questions such as: "What do you care most about in this situation? What does success look like from your point of view? What do you wish other factions and groups understood about you? What do you stand to lose if progress is made on this issue?"

▶ ONCE YOU DEEPLY UNDERSTAND WHERE THEY ARE COMING FROM, START WITH "YES-ABLE" PROPOSITIONS. List everyone who will be affected by a cause or decision.

▶ ONLY AFTER WORKING HARD TO UNDERSTAND THEM, BEGIN ASKING FOR THEIR FEEDBACK ON YOUR OPINIONS. Ask something of the other faction you are 99 percent sure they can agree to.

▶ DON'T SEE THINGS AS A ZERO SUM GAME. Pluralism is good. Don't try to annihilate the other faction. See the value in their thinking and work to blend into a shared purpose. Work together for the common good.

Mahatma Gandhi and Jawaharlal Nehru were both instrumental in India's long fight for freedom. Nehru's education and experience made him a man of the West, champion of parliamentary democracy and universal adult suffrage. Gandhi, on the other hand, had a more Eastern outlook, envisioning a society based on the life of Buddha and a village culture centered on manual work and individual sacrifice. The two were often at odds. Visions clashed. Strategies conflicted. However, they kept moving forward (differently, in the same direction) focused on what mattered most — freedom from Britain and releasing their people from the chains of poverty.

MAKE IT REAL
Q & A

I am an associate in a law firm and currently working on a very large project with two groups of stakeholders. Each group is positioning themselves to be right and, by the way they are treating each other, clearly don't think the other party has anything to offer. What needs to be done to get us all working toward one common goal?

- FACTION-FILLED FRAN

Dear Fran,

Take a good long look at the tips above. Invite someone to lunch. Listen really well. Ask about what really matters. Then have a similar conversation with someone from the other faction. Try to identify overlapping interests. Maybe you can come up with one thing both parties can agree on. If you can't come to a yes-able proposition on your own, bring the two factions together and make the case that there is value in identifying common interests. Ask each to talk about what they care about. Then help them identify overlaps.

Onward!

CHAPTER 16

ENERGIZE OTHERS

Create a Trustworthy Process

**Leadership isn't about the right answers —
but it is about process.**

In one way, that's a freeing notion. You don't have to have all the answers. If the process engages, honors and challenges people, you stand a greater chance of having the group discover what needs to be done. On the other hand, people get stuck if the process seems fishy, unpredictable or lacks transparency.

Progress on the challenges facing today's organizations takes time. People must do work they would rather avoid. It's a process, and the process must be trustworthy.

"SO IT'S BASICALLY A MATTER
OF EACH OF US DOING OUR JOB,
NOW, ISN'T IT?"

Don't confuse trustworthy with conflict-free. A trustworthy process doesn't mean there's an absence of tension. Rather, it's by working through the tension that people make progress.

And there is a difference between trusting everyone involved and a trustworthy process.

Rarely will people all completely trust each other, especially if you are convening a diverse group of stakeholders. Maybe the people you need to engage don't know each other well enough — or maybe they know each other too well — to fully trust. Maybe all the ice-breakers and teambuilding exercises in the world won't do the trick.

Building trust among people is a good thing. But the leadership idea here, the one that really helps energize others, is to create a trustworthy process.

One way to see this distinction is through the participants in our programs. They come together from different walks of life. We challenge them to immediately work together to help each other make progress on their own individual dilemmas. In their short time together, with tough expectations laid out before them, it is unrealistic, maybe impossible, to think they could establish any kind of full trust to work together.

What does happen, though, is that through a trustworthy and transparent process based on collaboration and confidentiality, people can dig deep, and fast, to share meaningful things with their new counterparts and help each other make progress.

WANT TO LEARN MORE ABOUT CREATING
A TRUSTWORTHY PROCESS?
Search for the Simon Sinek "Why good leaders
make you feel safe" talk on www.ted.com.

Leadership is more about the process challenges than the content challenges. You don't have to have the answers, but if the process engages, honors and challenges people, you stand a chance of having the group discover the right answers for its situation. All along the way, the process must be trustworthy.

Why? Because much is at stake. Remember, leadership is about change and change sometimes means loss. People stand to lose things — for real or just in their heads — if the change you are promoting succeeds. They are already on edge. A move they don't understand or that lacks transparency could send them over that edge.

HERE ARE A FEW EXAMPLES.

▶ A union president is promoting new models for paying teachers. The current "years of service plus education level salary grid" has been in place for decades, and that makes the teachers skeptical from the beginning. It will be nearly impossible to implement if teachers, parents, administrators, school board members, students and others don't trust the process.

▶ A civic official is spearheading an effort to generate generous economic incentives to lure businesses. The incentives will redirect taxpayer dollars from such things as streets, sidewalks and public safety to the private accounts of for-profit businesses. Community unrest may boil over if citizens don't feel the process for distributing incentives is above board.

▶ A group of employees longs for a better culture at work, a culture that promotes sharing, curiosity, learning and asking for help. Other employees are skeptical. They fear poor performance reviews if they ask for help and worry others will get promoted over them if they share knowledge. The culture won't change if the instigators can't figure out how to create more trust among the crew.

WHAT ARE CHARACTERISTICS OF A TRUSTWORTHY PROCESS?

- People are free to express ideas, thoughts and opinions.

- Those most affected are part of generating ideas and making decisions.

- People know where they fit in the process. They know what happened before and what's coming next.

- There is space and time to express vulnerability.

- Those in charge model openness to exploring new ideas.

- The lines of authority and non-authority become blurred as people work together.

- Higher-ups embrace failure as a learning opportunity, helping others deal with fear of making mistakes.

HOW DO YOU CREATE A TRUSTWORTHY PROCESS?

- **Ask open-ended questions.** Lots of them. Broad questions allow people to share what's on their minds. Use trust-building questions like: What concerns you the most about this issue? What would make this successful from your point of view? Of all the things we could do, what should we do?

- **Listen to understand.** Most of us listen just enough so we can reply. Forget about replying. Just understand. Discern the song beneath the words.

- **Be around.** If you are there, with the people, they'll have more chances to visit with you informally and formally. Being super-busy and running from meeting to meeting, event to event, creates an image of "I'm too busy to talk about what's on your mind."

- **Design the process together.** Ask others: How should we work on this issue? What's important to you about how we work on this?

- **Create multiple environments.** Take people to coffee to chat. Bring all the stakeholders together for collective discussion. Send out a survey. The more different types of environments made available, the more likely everyone will experience a type they are comfortable with.

- **Consider establishing group norms at the start of the work.** For example, "We agree to give honest feedback to one another to learn and grow. In return we agree not to take things personally. There will be no dancing around issues. Let's have a data-gathering mindset versus blame and fear of failing."

If you bring the right people together in constructive ways with good information, they will create authentic visions and strategies to address the shared concerns of their organization or community.

— *DAVID CHRISLIP*

MAKE IT REAL
Q & A

As a newly elected legislator, I'm concerned about what my district thinks now that the campaign is over. With all of the mud-slinging and distrust in politics nowadays, how can I get to work for people who already don't believe I will do a good job?

- **POLITICAL PABLO**

Dear Pablo,

It's rare to find an elected official focused on building a trustworthy process among their office and constituents. Congratulations! Getting elected with that kind of mindset is half the work! Gather eight to 10 people with a range of views. Ask what's most important. Ask what kind of citizen engagement they'd like to see. That's your first experiment. See what you learn and go from there. You can let us know how it goes by leaving a comment at www.yourleadershipedge.com.

Onward!

CHAPTER 17

ENERGIZE OTHERS

Speak to Loss

"People are afraid of change."

We've all heard that one before. It's the simplistic answer explaining lack of progress on what matters most.

The marketing department is stuck in its ways, unwilling to try something new. "They are afraid of change!"

The teachers aren't open to new methods and salary models. "They are afraid of change!"

Have you noticed how seldom we claim to be afraid of change ourselves? Maybe no one is actually afraid of change. Maybe we just think they are afraid.

A new term is in vogue in community and civic life: "CAVE people." You'll hear it in town hall meetings and at chamber of commerce mixers. CAVE stands for "citizens against virtually everything." Just about any place

"NEW SEATING WILL BE PERHAPS THE MOST VISIBLE DIFFERENCE YOU WILL SEE IN CHANGING FROM ONE HOUR DAYS WITH EIGHT HOURS OF BREAK TO EIGHT HOUR DAYS WITH ONE HOUR OF BREAK."

a group is trying to make something new happen in a community — build a park, pass a school bond issue, develop incentives to lure businesses — the proponents bemoan the CAVE people. "They are afraid of change! They are holding us back!"

We have yet to meet anyone who claims membership in the CAVE club. Perhaps complaints about CAVE people or marketing departments tap into our human nature to vilify others and let ourselves off the hook.

> *Our friend Marty Linsky, from the Kennedy School of Government at Harvard, says no one is afraid of change per se. What we fear is the loss that comes with change.*

Your grand idea doesn't look so grand to them. You see possibility. They see loss. You see hope. They see despair. You see progress. They see all kinds of problems that may or may not be connected (from your perspective) to the issue you care about.

Our experience suggests most of us don't understand the distinction between change and loss. Moreover, those of us working for a change do everything we can to focus energy away from negatives. We deny the potential losses and, if we can't get away with simple denial, we defend and make speeches about why those losses make sense.

Mobilizing others on tough challenges (aka exercising leadership) often requires us to "speak to loss."

WHAT DOES THAT LOOK LIKE?

▶ After a great deal of turnover in her church, a member organizes a meeting for parishioners and says, "I know we've experienced a great deal of change lately. And because we're not the pastor or church staff, we feel like the situation is out of our control. In fact, I've been frustrated myself and have even considered transferring to another church. The truth is, though, that I just care too much about this place and our community and, by your presence here tonight, I can tell you do too."

▶ Rather than only touting the perceived benefits of the new commercial development in town, the mayor also says, "And I understand this won't all be easy. Business owners will face new competition. I understand that in many ways this effort — especially in the short run — may make things harder for you. We are doing this to help the city grow overall. That growth should benefit everyone, but it might not feel like it right away."

▶ While speaking at the annual all-employee meeting, the CEO describes the gains the company will make because of increased efficiency and the streamlined production process. He also says, "These changes, while good for our bottom line, don't necessarily feel rosy all the time. New efficiencies mean fewer employees. Many of our colleagues and friends have been let go because of the streamlining. I would like to take some time now to hear how these changes are affecting you. What's been hard about all this change?"

WHY SHOULD YOU SPEAK TO LOSS?

- **To build trust.** Acknowledging the loss builds your credibility.

- **To help people get unstuck.** If people don't process their loss, it could get in the way of moving forward. Speaking about loss is not very comfortable, but it can generate new energy.

- **To validate their feelings.** People need to know that they are heard and that you care.

WHAT MAKES IT HARD?

- **It feels risky.** We are afraid, because we don't know what to expect. We are taught to be positive. At first, speaking to loss feels anything but positive.

- **We aren't used to uncertainty and conflict** and bringing up losses brings both to the surface. (See Chapter 8 for more related to this topic.)

- **We're responsible.** Often, we are the ones bringing on the loss and we would rather not "own" or be responsible for the others' feelings. Not only might we feel responsible for their loss, but once we acknowledge their loss, we may feel like we need to do something about it.

Dorothea Lange captured unforgettable images from the Depression and World War II on the homefront in America. Famous pieces include photographs such as "Migrant Mother," which captures the face, fortitude, pain and grit of Depression-era mothers, and photographs showing Japanese Americans pledging their allegiance to the United States minutes before being sent to internment camps. By taking images that show real loss unfolding in the country, Lange highlighted things that many may have preferred to go unnoticed but were important for people to understand.

HOW DO YOU "SPEAK TO LOSS"?

- **Speak directly to their loss.** Don't say, "I know how you feel," because you don't. But do acknowledge the loss. Describe the loss you see them experiencing.

- **Ask others to speak to their own loss.** Get them talking about it. Give the work back. Be careful to not jump in and start defending. For example, if you ask them the question, "What's been hard about all of this change?" resist the urge to respond to every comment. Instead, listen closely, ask questions if what they're saying doesn't make sense and thank them for sharing.

- **Share your own loss** as a way to create an environment where sharing loss is accepted and valued. Be authentic and vulnerable.

- **Do less rather than more.** Creating the opportunity for others to speak to loss does not require you to say much. Sometimes it's just about allowing more space. If this is something that is not the norm, you may need to create an environment where honest conversation can take place.

Our local nonprofit organization is getting ready to merge with the larger parent organization to save costs. Unfortunately, this means people will be shifting roles and, in some cases, losing their jobs. How can we cope with this transition in the coming months?

MAKE IT REAL
Q & A

- TED IN TRANSITION

Dear Ted,

This is a tough one and feels particularly personal given that people's jobs are at stake. So just start there. Acknowledge you all are in a difficult situation and you understand it's going to be hard to stay focused and keep working toward the organization's mission with so much uncertainty looming about.

Resist the urge to try to make it right. What do we mean? Don't try to tell them everything will be OK; you don't know that for certain. And don't try to talk about the organization's mission and purpose to motivate them to stick with it, as you will most likely drive them further away.

You might also be asking, "Why is it so hard to not jump in and start defending?" This can be incredibly difficult. Oftentimes, you might know more details about the decision that caused the change. Usually, these details help explain why the decision, no matter how hard, was the best choice. We defend as a way to share the information that can help level out the conversation — although as we've learned, it ends up not being the most effective way to do this. In our desire to not have conflict, we also defend to self-protect and justify that the pain someone else feels was worth the change we helped make happen.

So just be with them. Create the space for people to share what they are thinking. And be prepared that this may need to happen as a group, or it may need to happen one-on-one. Everyone experiences change differently, and the best thing you can do is be open, honest and present.

Onward!

CHAPTER 18

ENERGIZE OTHERS

Inspire a Collective Purpose

You can't make progress on adaptive challenges without inspiring a collective purpose. Leadership means finding ways to get more and more people to care. Amanda is part of a nonprofit organization that helps children learn through the arts. The organization is dedicated to inspiring a collective purpose among school administrators, teachers, parents and financial supporters. What's challenging is that each faction — administrators, teachers, parents, financial supporters — has its own values and loyalties.

For example, administrators value easy, low-cost programming that fits with their established curriculum. Teachers are loyal to the routine they create for their classes. Parents expect a quality education, and financial supporters want to know their dollars are being used in ways reflecting their values.

To be more than just a do-gooder arts organization, the board and staff must inspire a collective purpose among all the factions.

WHY IS IT IMPORTANT TO INSPIRE A COLLECTIVE PURPOSE? CONSIDER THESE SCENARIOS.

▶ A pastor's sermons on doing more for the poor are just rhetoric unless she convinces listeners to act differently.

▶ A nonprofit board member's concerns about the financial future of the organization are irrelevant unless she can get others, like board members and staff, to care too.

▶ A CEO's call for departments to appreciate each other more is mere management speak unless employees companywide embrace the idea.

▶ A young professional's frustration about the little opportunity for career advancement in his company is just a single complaint unless he can get others, such as the human resources department or senior staff, to care.

Efforts involving multiple factions tend to be like circles that all overlap just a bit (think of a Venn diagram). Each faction has its own purpose, and all those purposes have at least something in common that unites the factions and makes collective work possible.

So now, take the young professional from the example above. He might discover that the HR manager doesn't much care about advancement opportunities but does get fired up about the prospect of not having to train new people every year or two. He may learn the sales force cares deeply about employees generating leads from friends and family. The sales force knows young professionals are more likely to do that if they feel they can grow and succeed in the company. Stitching together these different purposes into a collective purpose becomes an exercise of leadership.

HOW DO YOU INSPIRE A COLLECTIVE PURPOSE?

▶ UNDERSTAND THE FACTIONS YOU NEED ON BOARD. What do they care about? How much do they care? What will it take to get them at the table? What are the connecting interests between their work and yours?

▶ ENGAGE THOSE FACTIONS EARLY AND OFTEN. Don't wait until you are desperate for their involvement. (Then it's all about what YOU need.) Rather, engage them over time, finding ways to help them advance what they care about.

▶ CARE AS MUCH ABOUT THEIR CAUSE AS YOURS. Otherwise, you are just using them to advance your effort. Contribute your time to their cause.

▶ IGNITE IMAGINATIONS. If you have convening power, build momentum by inviting everyone to dream about, contribute to and create a shared vision.

▶ BUILD TRUST ALONG THE WAY. Allow time for stakeholders to share stories and ask questions. Create space for people to be heard.

▶ MAKE THE GOALS ATTAINABLE. The purpose may be lofty — the work of a lifetime, perhaps. Keep people energized by breaking it into achievable chunks.

▶ TAKE ACTION. Nothing is less inspiring than a whole lot of talk and no action. Harness the momentum by starting to experiment before you have all the answers.

HOW DO YOU KNOW WHEN A COLLECTIVE PURPOSE EXISTS?

- Divergent factions have united behind one vision.
- A common language (abbreviations, jargon, etc.) arises among the group.
- You celebrate successes, large and small.
- The talents and connections of various groups get leveraged to make more progress.

Remember, inspiring a collective purpose doesn't mean everyone agrees about everything. Adaptive challenges need lots of people doing lots of things. No one idea will suffice. In adaptive work, it's often not possible to get all the stakeholders to agree to one specific plan of attack. It wouldn't be smart either because it would limit experimentation, providing fewer chances to learn what works.

Perhaps Ed's Aunt Kathleen — a Loretto nun whose life was dedicated to the common good — understood this best. At her funeral she was described as "someone who encouraged us not to conform, but to head in the same direction, differently." Sometimes, inspiring a collective purpose requires you to step back, look at the broader picture and find a purpose everyone can hold onto.

WANT TO LEARN MORE ABOUT INSPIRING A COLLECTIVE PURPOSE?

Watch closely as any political official works to cobble together votes to pass controversial legislation. The give and take of the legislative process is an explicit demonstration of what inspiring a collective purpose looks like.

For a different and more personal take, check out Stacy Horn's book "Imperfect Harmony: Finding Happiness Singing With Others."

MAKE IT REAL
Q & A

A recent neighborhood association meeting I attended basically just consisted of planning events like a community potluck and garage sale. This is great, but I feel like we could have a lot of power if we came together on an issue. How do we shift to that kind of thinking?

- NEIGHBORHOOD NORA

Dear Nora,

What is the adaptive challenge? What is the thing you are trying to mobilize people around?

Yes, you and your neighbors could have a lot of power, but not without a shared purpose. Start asking big, open-ended questions such as, "When you think about the future of our neighborhood, what concerns you the most?" Talk to enough people, listen carefully, and you'll soon determine the challenges crying out for more leadership. By engaging your neighbors in such an open-ended way, you will ignite imaginations and build trust. You'll be on your way to inspiring a collective purpose.

Onward!

The true measure of leadership must be that actions or interventions lead to progress. We define an intervention as an attempt by one or more people to make progress. To Intervene Skillfully is to do so consciously and purposefully. Skillful interventions help manage conflict by bringing it into the open and working through it in a productive way.

Making progress on adaptive challenges takes innovation and experimentation. As advocates for change, we must keep in mind that there's no way of knowing whether an intervention will work until we try it. If it works, great, then we move on to the next one. If it doesn't, we evaluate why, adjust the approach and try again. Change starts with someone who cares enough to work hard and take the inevitable, necessary risks.

PART 4

INTERVENE SKILLFULLY

CHAPTER 19

INTERVENE SKILLFULLY

Make Conscious Choices

To lead effectively you must see the options and make conscious choices to advance your purpose. There are two elements to this idea: "being conscious" and "making choices."

Being conscious

How often do you really make a conscious choice? Most of us go about our day doing more floating than choosing. Floating from one meeting to the next, one month to the next, one project to the next. Going through the routine. Not thinking much about it.

We "wake up" at the end of the month, the conclusion of a project or even toward the end of our life and wonder, "how did we get here?"

We make hundreds of choices every day (what to wear to this event, who to talk with during the break in meetings, which emails to respond to first, what items to remove from the to-do list, etc.), but few are deliberate and

"WE EAT BRAINS BECAUSE
BRAINS ARE FOR EATING. WHAT MORE
IS THERE TO THINK ABOUT?"

conscious. Few are strategic and purposeful. Most are unconscious and lack logic or strategy.

The number of conscious choices you make each day probably has some corollary to whether you are leading or not. Participants in our programs and experiences report they initially have trouble becoming more conscious about their choices when attempting to exercise leadership. Why?

HERE ARE A COUPLE REASONS:

▶ THEIR UNCONSCIOUS BEHAVIOR IS WORKING FOR THEM. For example: If you jump in at the first sign of a problem and "fix" things, it builds your ego and solidifies your identity as a "fixer," even if the better leadership behavior would be to keep diagnosing the situation.

▶ IT TAKES TIME. You need to slow down to see the choices coming. But everything in life goes faster and faster! It helps to recognize that leadership is abnormal behavior. It runs against the grain. It's rare, and for good reason. To make more conscious choices you'll need to take care of yourself, hold to purpose and choose among competing values. (Check out those chapters in this book.)

Making choices

During jury service, Ed was struck with how hard it was for some members of the jury to make a choice — guilty or not guilty. It was a murder case and a guilty verdict would result in a 30- to 40-year sentence. It was a complicated case, up until the point the prosecutors played a taped confession. Then it was pretty clear. He was guilty. And even with that evidence, three jurors struggled to make a choice. They couldn't present a clear argument that he was innocent. They were just crushed by the weight of the decision.

It's hard to lead if you can't get comfortable making choices — conscious choices, deliberate choices where you choose one thing over something else.

Making choices is hard when working on an adaptive challenge because there is seldom a clear choice. Nothing is 100 percent right or wrong, yes or no, good or bad.

When Ed was in the Legislature he rarely was ready to vote when the speaker of the House said, "The clerk will clear the rolls and the members will cast their votes," a phrase uttered several thousand times each term. Ed had to press the green (yes) or the red (no) button. There was no more delaying, deliberating or researching. Yes? No? Red? Green? On issues with adaptive elements, he rarely felt 100 percent certain.

It's hard to make choices in adaptive work, because each choice means we are deliberately elevating one thing we care about over something else we also care about. It doesn't feel good.

Here's a simple example from Amanda's family:

The unspoken rule for family visits is that the refrigerator should be stocked with food everyone enjoys — including a hearty supply of soda. To make changes for a healthier lifestyle, Amanda and her husband rarely have soda around the house anymore. They had a difficult choice to make with the impending arrival of her parents — to stock the fridge with soda or not?

Amanda's purpose was clear — try to make the healthy choice the easier choice for herself and her family. She thought about the many options for what to do. She could still purchase soda, just not as much. She could wait until they arrived and then decide. She could not buy it at all. After considering the options, she thought about the many interpretations her parents might make if she didn't have any soda available. They might be upset. She could look like she didn't prepare for their visit and risk their thinking the visit wasn't important — they weren't important. They could interpret her action as disrespect.

But her purpose was clear. She decided no soda.

Just a silly soda example, right? Wrong. The choice ran much deeper for Amanda. Making conscious choices that run against the norm is challenging.

"One's philosophy is not best expressed in words; it is expressed in the choices one makes ... and the choices we make are ultimately our responsibility."

— ELEANOR ROOSEVELT

HOW DO YOU KNOW WHEN YOU'VE MADE A CONSCIOUS CHOICE?

- Did you think about your action before jumping in?

- Did you stop to make a few observations and interpretations about the choice you were about to make?

- Did you feel the heat go up? (See Chapter 19 on Raise the Heat.)

HOW DO YOU MAKE CONSCIOUS CHOICES?

- **Think like a scientist.** Get in the habit of creating hypotheses. "If I do _____, I think _____ will happen." Then test your hypothesis and reflect on it.

- **Get really clear on your purpose.** Stephen Covey says, "The main thing is to keep the main thing the main thing." What's your main thing? Knowing it will help you make conscious choices to advance it.

- **Create a menu of options before you choose.** Don't go with your first idea. Create three or four choices you could make, evaluate and then choose.

WANT TO LEARN MORE ABOUT MAKING CONSCIOUS CHOICES?

Read "The Power of Habit: Why We Do What We Do in Life and Business" by Charles Duhigg. We love the idea of the "habit loop" in Chapter 1 and suspect that making conscious choices in leadership has something to do with rewiring that loop.

President Abraham Lincoln's "drafts" folder would be pretty full if he had email. After his death his staff found dozens of letters written months or years earlier, all fully drafted, folded in envelopes and addressed. The letters were harsh rebukes of generals, irate missives to other officials or constituents. The letters show that our 16th president had a temper. The key is, the letters were never sent. By writing them and tucking them away in a desk drawer, Lincoln managed his triggers. He created a buffer between his emotional reaction (which led to the writing of the letter) and his action (choosing not to send the letters).

MAKE IT REAL
Q & A

I just started a new job. I'm known for jumping right in to projects and getting really involved. How can I be most effective as "the new guy" and also not get in over my head too quickly?

- JUMPING JAMAL

Dear Jamal,

A sure recipe for getting in over your head is jumbling up the technical and adaptive elements of your job and treating them all the same.

It's time for some conscious choices. Slow down. Diagnose the situation. Give yourself a little time before you intervene.

What about your job is technical? Make a list. Get on those technical things right away. Use your expertise and authority to solve those problems.

Now, what is adaptive? Make another list. Begin to engage others about the items on that list. Use questions such as: How do you see this dynamic? What concerns you the most about this? What gets in the way of progress on that?

And Jamal! Keep in mind that simply by making those two lists you will already be practicing "making conscious choices"! Well done.

Onward!

CHAPTER 20

INTERVENE SKILLFULLY

Raise the Heat

Making progress on tough issues often requires "raising the heat" to get ourselves and others to do difficult work. Until there is enough pressure (heat) people just won't act.

Raising the heat means doing something big or small to compel people to act — to make it more uncomfortable not to address the issue than to live with the issue.

This is true of life in general. Too many of us don't save for retirement until the pressure is on. We put off confronting a friend or relative about a tough situation.

WANT TO LEARN MORE ABOUT RAISING THE HEAT?

Read "Leadership on the Line: Staying Alive Through the Dangers of Leading" by Ron Heifetz and Marty Linsky.

SO HOW DO YOU RAISE THE HEAT?

▶ SAY WHAT OTHERS WON'T.

- State the consequences of inaction.
- Name the elephant in the room.
- Take the temperature. Name it. (See Chapter 4.)
- Speak from the heart. (See Chapter 21.)
- Offer different interpretations. (See Chapter 3.)
- Make a statement about your own frustration: "I am not sure where to go here, but I am frustrated with our lack of progress" or "I am concerned about how quickly we are jumping to solutions."

▶ CREATE STRUCTURES AND ASSIGN RESPONSIBILITY.

- Write down responsibilities and timelines, and include those in future agendas.
- Define the roles of individuals and organizations involved in the challenge, thus urging responsibility where it's needed most.
- Grab the bull by the horns and declare a way forward. Action often raises the heat and forces people to engage more fully.

▶ DISRUPT NORMS.

- Use silence. Don't jump in and answer questions or smooth over tough issues. Let others do the work.
- Allow more time. Tough issues will surface if you let a group stew.
- Ask powerful, open-ended questions.
- Ask someone directly for input.
- Interrupt someone who has taken up a lot of air time. Ask them to hold their comments to create some space for those we have not yet heard from.
- Give the work back. (See Chapter 22.)
- Bring somebody new to the discussion. (See Chapter 13.)

▶ ARTICULATE THE OBVIOUS.

- Point out potential losses or ask what they might be.
- Compare and contrast what is going on.
- Name the values at the heart of the conflict.

▶ KNOW WHEN TO RAISE THE HEAT. LOOK FOR THESE CLUES.

- You are the only one doing the work.
- Urgent action is required.
- There is an elephant in the room. You know because people keep mentioning it to you in private.
- You aren't satisfied with the rate of progress.
- You find yourself disengaged from something you care about.
- Important questions aren't being addressed.
- Your gut tells you the group is going in the wrong direction.
- Just a couple of people are doing the work, with most folks staying silent.

"When you can't make them see the light, make them feel the heat."

— *RONALD REAGAN*

... we have learned to pile on the logs,
then we can come to see how
it is fuel, and absence of the fuel
together, that makes fire possible.
We only need lay a log
lightly from time to time.
A fire
grows
simply because the space is there,
with openings
in which the flame
that knows just how it wants to burn
can find its way.

— *JUDY BROWN, "FIRE"*

So you've raised the heat. What do you do now?

MODERATE THE TEMPERATURE. If it is getting too hot, you may need to help people get back down to a manageable level. Sharpening your facilitation skills will help.

PREPARE FOR THE HEAT TO BE RAISED ON YOU. Now that you have raised the heat, consider the ideas in the Manage Self section to help you anticipate your own triggers or lean in to uncertainty and conflict.

EVALUATE THE RESULTS OF RAISING THE HEAT. Debrief the group about what happened. What worked? What would you do differently? Was it worth it? Have you made progress toward your purpose?

Lessons from History

RAISING THE HEAT

Is there a better example of raising the heat than Rosa Parks refusing to give up her seat for a white passenger on that Montgomery bus in December 1955? Her refusal and subsequent arrest led to the Montgomery bus boycott, which eventually led to the integration of the city's bus system and served as a focal point for the civil rights movement.

Every month for three years I've attended committee meetings for an organization I care deeply about. Lately, it feels like we're stuck. There's little engagement, and it seems like we're just going through the motions. Frankly, if this is all we're going to do, I have other ways to spend my time. I'm not ready to give up quite yet. So I'm wondering, what can I do to help us break out of this rut?

- **REAGAN IN A RUT**

Dear Reagan,

You do have better ways to spend your time. Your committee is accomplishing nothing, except for the illusion of being a functioning group. We are sure there are all sorts of adaptive challenges present, but the heat is so low nothing is happening.

Try one or more of these heat-raising ideas:

1. Keep track of how many people are active in the meeting and then say something along these lines: "I've noticed there are 17 people here, but only three have spoken. Is that what a high-functioning group looks like?"

2. Raise the bar. Suggest that the committee adopt a lofty goal and then evaluate itself against that goal.

3. Simply ask, "How would we know if we are being effective?"

4. And then there is the nuclear option: Let folks know you believe you have better ways to spend your time and you'll quit the committee if the group doesn't get more engaged.

Onward!

P.S. Don't go "nuclear" unless you are ready to follow through!

CHAPTER 21

INTERVENE SKILLFULLY

Speak from the Heart

Robert Greenleaf ushered in a new way to think of leaders: as servants. He coined the term "servant leadership" and has helped millions of people think differently about their role as a manager or authority figure. Those moved by his ideas would no longer think it was the job of their employees to serve them. It would be the other way around.

This approach lifted the spirits of employees and managers alike. Uplifted spirits led to better performance, which resulted in success for the organization or company. Greenleaf, the longtime AT&T executive, was on to something.

The notion of "speak from the heart" connects with this wonderful idea of servant leadership. The idea here is to speak from your heart in a way that connects to the hearts of the people you are trying to lead. A more complete name for this idea would be "speak from your heart TOWARD their heart." It is speaking with a purpose in mind. It is communicating your values at a level that connects with what the other person cares deeply about.

The key to "speaking from the heart" is that it's about them, not you.

What makes it hard to speak from the heart?

It's hard to do this if you don't have a genuine care and concern for those you are engaging. This is the root of Greenleaf's servant leadership idea. Leadership — different from management — is about helping people transcend their current state. You'll struggle to speak from the heart if you focus on what YOU want. Instead, focus on — and speak to — THEIR aspirations.

"Speaking from the heart" is a leadership behavior when you make it a strategic choice, an intervention designed to mobilize others. It is emotion with purpose. The exercise of leadership is often about finding connecting interests among various factions. Picture a singer holding people in rapture. The poetry of the words, the emotion of the music. A really good singer has a way of capturing the audience, enveloping listeners in the song and its story.

You'll be more likely to engage people in tough adaptive challenges if you demonstrate your connection — heart to heart — with them.

WANT TO LEARN MORE ABOUT SPEAKING FROM THE HEART?

Read "The Story Factor: Inspiration, Influence and Persuasion Through the Art of Storytelling" by Annette Simmons for ideas about how to use stories to speak from your heart.

Lessons from History

It's hard to find a better example than Dr. Martin Luther King Jr. when it comes to speaking from the heart. His words were and are powerful because they connect with the hopes and dreams of the people listening. He wasn't trying to get his audience to value new things. Rather, he was connecting to what they already valued and helping them understand the importance of standing up for those values.

U.S. Rep. John Lewis in "A Call to Conscience: The Landmark Speeches of Dr. Martin Luther King, Jr." describes King's words at the end of the march from Selma to Birmingham.

"When Dr. King gave his address on that Thursday afternoon he spoke from his heart and the depth of his soul. He spoke for all of us. Dr. King called upon the conscience of a nation. In his moving and eloquent address, Dr. King urged us to march on."

HOW DO YOU SPEAK FROM THE HEART?

▶ FIRST, USE BASIC COMMUNICATION SKILLS. Understand the environment, make eye contact and actively listen.

▶ KNOW WHAT OTHERS CARE ABOUT, WHAT'S IN THEIR HEARTS. Ask questions: What do you care about? What matters to you? Why is this important to you? How would you feel if this was successful?

▶ TELL THEM YOU CARE ABOUT THEIR FUTURES, THEIR HOPES AND DREAMS.

▶ CONSIDER SHARING A BRIEF STORY WITH PURPOSE that allows you to connect to things they care about.

▶ SPEAK OUT OF PASSION, NOT BECAUSE YOU ARE EMOTIONALLY TRIGGERED. Feel the emotion, compose yourself and think through what you are going to share. A moment's awareness allows you to be strategic about speaking from the heart.

MAKE IT REAL
Q & A

The board of our small community hospital has lately been focused more on trying to turn a profit than on the mission of why we exist. They want graphs and number charts when we're making our case about the things we need, but it just doesn't seem to be getting to the core of what our hospital needs right now. How do I get through to them?

- HANNAH THE HOSPITAL CEO

Dear Hannah,

Being a board member of a small community hospital surely isn't a lucrative financial position. Odds are those board members, deep down, joined the board in the first place because of the mission of the organization.

Ask a different board member each meeting to speak for three to five minutes about why the hospital is important to them and why they said "yes" to serving on the board. You'll create the conditions for members to speak from the heart. Building this into your board routine will ensure a connection at every meeting to what matters most.

Onward!

P.S. Make sure you give board members a few days' notice to prepare to speak.

CHAPTER 22

INTERVENE SKILLFULLY

Give the Work Back

All you type-A personalities out there need to pay close attention to this.

Leadership is as much about what you are not doing as what you are doing.

Too many of us, in our quest to solve problems and save the day, assume we are the ones who need to do the work. Maybe we hold the fancy title of CEO or president and assume that, by virtue of our role, we are supposed to step forward to identify the problem and the solution. Or perhaps we don't have an authority role, but we just have a knack for solving tough problems. People naturally turn to us for help. We listen and then we fix. It's what we do. It makes people happy and builds our ego at the same time. Perfect!

And here again is why knowing the difference between adaptive challenges and technical problems is so crucial. One job of those with authority (formal or informal) is to solve technical problems.

"OKAY, NOW WHAT?"

But adaptive challenges can't be solved, or even fully identified, by authority alone. A CEO or manager can instigate things, can use his or her authority to focus attention and provoke thinking, but eventually the people with the problem must get their hands dirty.

> *Adaptive challenges require the involvement and commitment of stakeholders. You make that happen by giving the work back.*

HERE ARE SOME HYPOTHETICAL EXAMPLES.

▶ The culture of a university is unproductive. It lacks innovation and collaboration. The university president can hope and wish for culture change but can't automatically make it happen. If it's about the culture, it's about the people themselves needing to change.

▶ A community is unhealthy. Obesity and malnutrition are increasing. Depression too. It affects the workforce and economy. A health-oriented organization — the medical society or a philanthropy — can spend its days focusing on the issue, but progress will be made only when residents make different choices about diet, exercise and lifestyle.

▶ The biggest concern facing a manufacturing company is the disconnect between plant workers and executives (overalls versus suits). Even when the senior executive and foreman agree on the problem, they can't solve it on their own. Men and women throughout the company actually have to engage and be open to changing relationships with one another.

"Giving the work back" versus "delegating"

Don't confuse this idea with delegation. Both are important, but delegation is an act of authority. Giving the work back is an act of leadership. It's not about spreading the work by assigning tasks. "Giving the work back" is about getting people deeply involved. It is creating the space to allow others to exercise leadership.

Delegation is a transfer of authority. Giving the work back is a sharing of responsibility.

For simplicity's sake, imagine that any adaptive challenge has only three phases.

Phase one is problem identification. What's the issue? What's going on? What's not satisfactory? What's the gap between where we are and where we want to go?

Phase two is solution identification. Of all the things we could do, what should we do? What's the best way to proceed? What will we value most?

Phase three is solution implementation. Who will do what, when and how? When will we report back? How will we stay in communication? How will we keep learning as we try one solution and then another?

Our experience suggests that most people don't "give the work back" until phase three, and then it's little more than delegating to get stuff done or a lame attempt to make it appear that people were involved from the beginning.

It is a leadership behavior to give the work back. And when facing an adaptive challenge, the best time to give the work back is in phases one and two.

GIVING THE WORK BACK IN PHASE ONE
AND PHASE TWO LOOKS LIKE THIS.

- Asking lots of questions: When you think about the future of this project, what concerns you the most? What's going to keep us from being successful? What holds us back? What are the hidden issues?

- Convening diverse factions to wrestle with those types of questions.

- Not initially offering solutions if you are in authority. See if solutions emerge.

- Talking less and listening more.

- Asking divergent groups to work together to develop a one-pager that describes the challenges (in phase one) or potential solutions (in phase two).

GIVING THE WORK BACK IN
PHASE THREE LOOKS LIKE THIS.

- Continuing to ask questions: What challenges are you facing? Where are we getting the most traction? What has surprised you? What does it mean?

- Convening diverse factions to share learning and making decisions about where to allocate resources.

- Being available for support but not jumping in to save foundering people.

- Celebrating successes, large and small.

- Helping people see failure as progress (We've learned something!).

- Looking for connections and identifying resources that could make the work easier.

- Reminding people to take care of themselves by getting enough rest, good food, exercise and laughter.

WHY MUST YOU GIVE THE WORK BACK?

- Unlike technical problems, adaptive challenges cannot be solved by authority alone.

- Tough challenges demand many perspectives. You can't rely on authority to represent everyone.

- Engaging others encourages those differing views to surface.

- It stimulates commitment and creativity and makes it more likely that a collective vision will emerge.

- It creates buy-in from people authentically engaged in the process.

Our experience suggests that giving the work back is one of the more difficult leadership behaviors. It runs counter to our culture, which says authority figures are responsible for solving tough challenges. Those in authority buy into it ("Yes, I am the one in charge and must save the day!") and those not in authority collude in it ("It's not my fault, I'm not in charge!"). Those with authority get a bigger ego. Those without authority avoid responsibility.

WHEN SHOULD YOU GIVE THE WORK BACK?

- When you are the only one working on the adaptive challenge.

- When you feel overwhelmed by the challenge.

- When people turn to you for answers instead of taking risks or working with others.

- When there are people who should be engaged who aren't involved yet.

- When others are more qualified to handle the work.

MAKE IT REAL

Q & A

As a company that is quickly growing from a small to medium-sized organization, management is realizing we need to start developing some of our lower-level employees into taking more initiative. How do I relinquish control and delegate some of my work — isn't that giving the work back?

- **MUHAMMAD THE MANAGER**

Dear Muhammad,

Yours is a clear adaptive challenge, because you can't force them to take more initiative. You can't make the choice for them. They must choose to take more initiative.

Instead of deciding to relinquish control and delegate some of your work, first talk with the employees about the challenges they see related to company growth. Ask them what makes it hard to take initiative in the company. Keep digging. My bet is they could develop ideas and strategies that would lead to more of their colleagues stepping up.

Onward!

CHAPTER 23

INTERVENE SKILLFULLY

Act Experimentally

Leadership requires you to get comfortable with failure.

A scientist trying to cure cancer doesn't fret over every failed experiment. She learns from it to inform the next experiment. Big challenges — adaptive challenges — have no clear solution. Progress is made when you take an experimental approach.

Legend has it Thomas Edison failed 10,000 times trying to create the light bulb. He later said, "I have not failed. I've just found 10,000 ways that won't work." Just like in the research lab, each leadership experiment brings new information that can shape future experiments. Acting experimentally implies you are doing lots of experiments, and that mindset is useful in guiding your overall approach to adaptive work.

You can't exercise leadership without experimenting. You need to develop the stomach to try something, fail, learn and experiment some more.

HERE ARE A COUPLE EXAMPLES.

▶ A newly elected governor feels pressure to stimulate the economy after a recession. He promotes one specific approach to stimulate the economy, invests huge resources and promises big returns. He is running just one big experiment despite the reality that no one actually knows the exact way to stimulate a state economy in the 2010s.

▶ A middle manager is asked to improve the productivity of two large units in an organization. It's been a long-running problem and, over the years, countless experts have tried to make it go away.

The CEO suggests merging units. Rather than run with that idea, the middle manager gathers key people from both teams (experiment 1) and asks them how to improve productivity (experiment 2).

She learns the merger idea scares the heck out of people and that the threat of merger has actually caused a productivity drop. Rather than a whole merger, she creates a short-term task force made up of members from both teams to work on a discreet project (experiment 3).

She wants to test how they work together. She also announces a one-time bonus for all teams meeting a new productivity metric (experiment 4).

Finally, she creates an informal cross-unit group to meet regularly to discuss what they are learning from the experiments (experiment 5).

The second example describes what acting experimentally looks like. The first describes foolishness. Everything is riding on the governor's experiment. A better approach would be to launch a series of experiments in the first year, testing different approaches in different parts of the state. Consolidate the learning from those experiments and make bigger experiments in years two and three and so forth.

In contrast to the middle manager's approach (several small experiments building over time with no possibility for catastrophic failure), if the governor's strategy fails, it could take years, perhaps a generation, to fully recover.

HOW DO YOU ACT EXPERIMENTALLY?

▶ DETERMINE HOW MUCH YOU CARE. Are you willing to fail? Is what you're thinking about worth experimenting on? The more you care, the more you will be willing to experiment.

▶ START CAUTIOUSLY. Begin with less risky experiments where you are pretty sure of the outcome. Then move to situations where the outcome is more in doubt and more important.

▶ TAKE A LESSON FROM SCIENCE. Ground your experiment in a clear purpose. Know what you expect will happen and then test your assumptions.

▶ GET STARTED. Set a date. Set a time. Get specific on the "Who? What? When? Where? Why? and How?" to hold you accountable.

▶ DEBRIEF. Pause between experiments to determine what you learned and how it ties to your purpose. What did you learn if it was successful? What did you learn if it failed?

▶ MAKE EXPERIMENTATION YOUR STANDARD OPERATING PROCEDURE. Over time, acting experimentally will become routine in situations demanding leadership.

Why is this difficult?

"Failure is bad, very bad." We are taught from an early age to strive for success. Experiments have the potential to fail. The risk makes us sick to our stomachs.

"I want success, and I want it now!" In a results-oriented society, we value immediate success over progress toward a long-term goal. There is no way around it; leadership on adaptive challenges takes time and requires experimentation.

FIVE WAYS TO HELP OTHERS
ACT EXPERIMENTALLY.

1. JUST USE THE WORD. When trying to find solutions, start saying things like "Well, one experiment we could try would be ..." or "What do you think we would learn if we tried this experiment ..." Over time you'll create a culture of experimentation.

2. REDEFINE FAILURE. Let everyone know that success or failure is not about the outcome of the experiment, it's about how much we learn — and don't just redefine your words, make sure your actions match up as well.

3. MODEL EXPERIMENTATION. Tell colleagues about your experiments. Share successes, failures and what you hope to learn.

4. VALUE LEARNING. Ask open-ended questions that reveal what others have learned. Celebrate discoveries and small successes.

5. LEVERAGE YOUR AUTHORITY. If you are in a position of authority, use it to show you believe progress on tough challenges is made with a series of experiments. Use your authority to focus attention on areas ripe for experimentation.

"The country needs and, unless I mistake its temper, the country demands bold, persistent experimentation. It is common sense to take a method and try it: If it fails, admit it frankly and try another. We need enthusiasm, imagination and the ability to face facts, even unpleasant ones, bravely. We need the courage of the young. Yours is not the task of making your way in the world, but the task of remaking the world which you will find before you. May every one of us be granted the courage, the faith and the vision to give the best that is in us to that remaking!"

— *FRANKLIN DELANO ROOSEVELT, 1932*

MAKE IT REAL
Q&A

Senior management at our company has been doing a lot of micro-managing lately. I'm trying to keep a project moving forward but keep getting stopped when I have to get approval or explain something. What can I do so I don't keep getting slowed down?

- FAST FREDDY

Dear Freddy,

Here are a few experiments to try.

1. Create a clear "midpoint" for your project and ask your manager whether it's OK if you don't check in until you get to that midpoint.

2. Share your observation, and ask why they think it's happening. Don't assign meaning to what is happening or blame senior management.

3. Ask your manager what parts of the project concern her most and what you could do to alleviate concerns ahead of time.

4. Suggest to your manager that you both focus on outcomes rather than your activities. See if you can get her to hold you accountable just for those outcomes.

Each of those small experiments helps you learn more about your situation and how to be effective. Experiment away!

Onward!

CHAPTER 24

INTERVENE SKILLFULLY

Hold to Purpose

There's a scene in the movie "42" when Jackie Robinson is about to become the first African-American to join a major league baseball team. He and Brooklyn Dodgers' general manager Branch Rickey are talking about what life will be like for Robinson. Rickey is being harsh and straightforward, using tough language and making sure Robinson understands just how brutal people will be toward him and his family. Rickey is stressing that under no circumstances can Robinson retaliate, that the public would accuse him of losing his cool and say HE was the cause of trouble. Triggered and emotional, Robinson blurts out, "What? You want a player that doesn't have the courage to fight back?" Rickey looks Robinson in the eye and says, "No! I want a player that has the courage NOT to fight back!"

Rickey was clear about purpose and wanted to make sure Robinson was too. He knew getting knocked off purpose would ruin the effort. You run the same risk with your leadership effort. It's always challenging to stay focused on what you are trying to accomplish.

Holding to purpose is about maintaining focus on what you value and want to accomplish.

Distractions are everywhere. We have needs (to be liked, save the day, stay employed, etc.) that can knock us off purpose. Opponents will try to knock us off track. They'll do it by attacking our vulnerabilities. Holding to purpose is to leadership what keeping your gloves up is to boxing. When a boxer's gloves go down and can no longer protect his head, a knockout isn't long off. When we get knocked off purpose, our efforts fizzle.

PURPOSE EXISTS ON MANY LEVELS AND INCLUDES:

- Life purpose
- Family purpose
- Career purpose
- Organization purpose
- Project purpose
- Committee purpose
- Meeting purpose
- Discussion purpose

Holding to purpose is critical in all of those dimensions.

HERE ARE A COUPLE EXAMPLES.

▶ Amanda and others at her church wanted to create more opportunity for young adults to socialize together. Their purpose was social interaction. Knowing their purpose became increasingly helpful. Occasionally, members would try to take the group in a different direction, turning it into a study group or theology discussion. Because there was a strong sense of purpose, though, people could speak up and remind everyone of the group's purpose. While some conversations felt difficult, the purpose provided direction.

▶ Ed's friend was elected to the Legislature on a pro-education platform. Her purpose was to use her new authority to increase funding for education. Three months into her first session Ed asked what she had accomplished on the education front. She went on and on about all the committee meetings she had to attend on all sorts of matters having nothing to do with education. She had been so busy she hadn't found time to work on education. Somewhere early in those three months she quit holding to purpose.

WANT TO LEARN MORE ABOUT HOLDING TO PURPOSE?

Read "Insanely Simple: The Obsession that Drives Apple's Success" by Ken Segall. The book makes the case that simplicity is a key to holding to purpose.

WHAT CAN YOU DO TO HELP YOURSELF AND OTHERS "HOLD TO PURPOSE"?

▶ **Get clear about the difference between purpose and strategies.** Your purpose should stay the same, but strategies can and will change. Be loyal to your purpose. Be flexible with your strategies.

▶ **Keep a "not-to-do" list.** Put things on there that you feel tempted to do but don't align with your purpose.

▶ **Figure out what you need to do each day to fulfill your life purpose.** For example, Ed has eight things he tries to do every day: pray, read, eat well, exercise, review finances, spend time with family, plan his day, and send a friend or family member a note. Doing those things day in and day out helps Ed stay centered and holding to purpose.

▶ **Don't just float in and out of meetings and discussions with others.** Be intentional. Write down notes to yourself about your purpose for any given meeting or discussion. Spend a minute or two before meetings reflecting on what your purpose is in that meeting.

▶ **Debrief and reflect.** After engaging with others, ask yourself if you accomplished your purpose. Where did you nail it? Where did you go wrong?

"When going through hell, keep going."
—*WINSTON CHURCHILL*

MAKE IT REAL
Q & A

Last year my church decided to start viewing church as more than just showing up on Sundays. Our purpose was and is to cultivate a more faithful way of being for all members. We decided "church" could take place anytime, anywhere. I was on the committee that supported this shift in thinking, and since starting to share it, we have received a lot of backlash. I truly believe in this stance, but the criticism is high. How do I not waver?

- WAVERING WANDA

Dear Wanda,

Backlash and criticism are par for the course when exercising leadership. Get used to it. You won't waver if (1) you truly value this new direction and (2) you protect yourself from getting knocked off track.

However, remember the difference between purpose and the current strategy. Your purpose is to cultivate a more faithful way of being for all members. Your current strategy is the decision regarding church anytime, anywhere. There could be multiple strategies to accomplish your purpose. Don't become overly loyal to this one.

Keep focused on your goal. Share your purpose openly with others. Read the consternation you're experiencing about the strategy carefully. Don't let a misguided strategy sink your overall purpose.

Onward!

ONWARD!

BY ED O'MALLEY

I am writing this brief conclusion just hours after returning home from two days at Harvard University. My friend and mentor Marty Linsky (who is mentioned often throughout this book) invited me to join Ron Heifetz and other Harvard faculty as they worked with 70 individuals from Argentina, Ireland, Jordan, Lithuania, Canada, Trinidad and Tobago, Australia, the United States and elsewhere.

They were there to learn about mobilizing others to make progress on daunting, adaptive challenges. They were there to learn about adaptive leadership.

It was a privilege to be with these wonderful people from around the world. They have accomplished success beyond the imagination of many. All of them are in the field of "leadership development." They are teachers and authors, consultants and coaches. They run consulting firms and colleges.

These "experts" in leadership came together to learn about their "leadership edge." They understand all of us have a leadership edge. None of us is competent at exercising leadership all of the time. We can all get better.

I was invited to explain what I've been up to these past eight years in Kansas, to explain our efforts at the Kansas Leadership Center to spread the ideas you've been reading about here to all corners of our state, and beyond.

The objective of this book is to spread the ideas further. It's meant to be a resource for participants in our programs and people who would never think to attend a program. Ultimately, this book represents our belief that people from Kansas to Kathmandu all have the potential to exercise leadership, no matter their role or title, but that doing so puts you at the edge of your competence.

It's scary out there on the edge. You never know when you are about to step too far. The ideas here help. They encourage you to step toward your edge on behalf of whatever you care most about. They strengthen you as you live on that edge, experimenting and working with others to bring about change. And they protect you from falling off, from getting in too deep.

Working with those fine, talented, successful people at Harvard reminds me that this work — the work of building the capacity to lead — is hard for all of us.

The world — the whole darn thing or just your little piece of it — needs more people who know how to exercise leadership.

If you've read this far, it's safe to officially welcome you to the edge. Welcome to the edge of your competence and the edge of possibilities that exist for your organization, company or community!

We know change doesn't just happen
if you wish for it by clicking your heels
(we're from Kansas, we should know).
Change happens if enough people
exercise leadership.

*Here's what you
can do next:*

1.

EXPERIENCE YLE ONLINE
www.yourleadershipedge.com

Subscribe to gain "anytime" access to videos, short stories, video chats, coaching tips and a community of people exercising leadership. Designed for self-paced leadership development, anyone with an Internet connection can access YLE from anywhere around the world.

2.

CONNECT WITH US

We're always available to talk leadership. Continue the conversation, join us for an in-person training, or come by for a visit:
yle@kansasleadershipcenter.org

Kansas Leadership Center
325 E Douglas Ave
Wichita, KS 67202
316.712.4950
www.kansasleadershipcenter.org

ACKNOWLEDGMENTS

Exercising leadership, as you'll read in these pages, cannot be done alone, much like the creation of this book. "Your Leadership Edge" is the result of many people, lots of breakfast conversations and wonderful ideas coming together to inform the advice and best practices throughout this book.

First and foremost, we thank the many alumni of our programs and friends of KLC who, over the years, have participated in our On the Balcony phone calls, attended focus groups for this book and submitted responses to evaluations that helped us better understand these ideas in a very practical way. Each chapter in this book has a "Make it Real Q&A" section. While the names and circumstances are fabricated, each question comes from real challenges our alumni face in the real world.

We are also thankful for our KLC family who spent hours coming up with movies, history examples or general critiques of early drafts. The KLC board, faculty, coaches and staff all have done the work of bringing these ideas to life. It is truly a joy to work with some of the best and brightest people around every day. A particular thank you to Julia Fabris McBride and Mike Matson for their editing and feedback, and Amy Nichols for creative direction and production management. And to our extended family who make us look good and remind us to have a little fun: our graphic designer Clare McClaren, cartoonist Pat Byrnes and editors Brian Whepley, Susie Fagan and Shannon Littlejohn.

Last, but not least, our utmost appreciation goes to the Kansas Health Foundation, for without their vision and willingness to push beyond their own leadership edge to create KLC, none of this would be possible.

ABOUT THE AUTHORS

ED O'MALLEY is the president and CEO of the Kansas Leadership Center. A former state legislator and gubernatorial aide, O'Malley founded the Kansas Leadership Center in 2007 and co-authored three other books including *When Everyone Leads* and *For The Common Good.*

AMANDA CEBULA is an Adjunct Instructor at Kansas State University. She served as the director of project development and business development at the Kansas Leadership Center from 2012-2017.